From Disability
to Possibility

From Disability
to Possibility

The Power of Inclusive Classrooms

Patrick Schwarz

Foreword by **Kylene Beers**

HEINEMANN
Portsmouth, NH

Heinemann
361 Hanover Street
Portsmouth, NH 03801–3912
www.heinemann.com

Offices and agents throughout the world

Library of Congress Cataloging-in-Publication Data
Schwarz, Patrick.
  From disability to possibility : the power of inclusive classrooms / Patrick Schwarz.
    p. cm.
  Includes bibliographical references.
  ISBN 0-325-00993-7 (alk. paper)
  1. Inclusive education—United States.   2. Learning disabled children—Education—United States.   I. Title.
LC1201.S38 2006
371.9'046—dc22   2006007447

Editor: Harvey Daniels
Production: Lynne Costa
Cover and interior designs: Joni Doherty Design
Cover photograph: ©Phil Date
Typesetter: TechBooks
Manufacturing: Steve Bernier

Printed in the United States of America on acid-free paper
10   09   08   EB   5

For Katie and Haley

You have opened my eyes
to a powerful perspective about learning and life

You are the inspiration for this book

Contents

Foreword

Be forewarned: This book grabs you, keeps you, and takes you in directions you had not expected. If you've ever taught a child with a disability, one direction this book will take you is right back to that child. You will finish a chapter and walk away to do something else, think of something else, attend to something else, but you won't be able to do it because Patrick Schwarz's descriptions of Sam or Gavin or Zach or Elizabeth will nudge at you. The Sam you'll meet in this book was my Ben, and I hadn't thought of Ben in years. This book brought him back to me.

* * *

I met Ben's mom before I met Ben. She showed up in my seventh-grade classroom a few days before school was to begin. Small, quiet, and determined, she was relentless in her expectations for what I would do for Ben. "He'll need all printed material, whether from the textbook or novels, reprinted in larger font and double-spaced. He'll need all worksheets redone in large font. Plus, all worksheets need to be in black ink," she said, unfazed that the school ran on purple ditto and there was only one copy machine in the entire school and that was only for the principal. "And if you put anything on the overhead projector," she continued, pointing to my main instructional tool, "you'll need to provide that for him on paper, also in large font, black ink, double-spaced."

I stopped her there and asked her to explain what she meant by anything. I couldn't begin to imagine how to get the stories in our literature anthology or the novels we would be reading retyped in large font, double-spaced, so I decided to skip that and focus on what she wanted done with transparencies for the overhead projector. I was thinking how often I turned students' essays into transparencies so we could look at what they had written. I was thinking of how often I used blank transparencies to record what students were saying during discussions, so we'd have a visible record of the talk as it emerged. I was thinking of how many times during a single class I would scribble notes in the margins of transparencies. I was thinking this woman was expecting the impossible. I politely tried to explain how this would be difficult.

"For whom?" she asked.

"Excuse me?" I replied.

"For whom will it be difficult?" she said. I didn't like the direction this was going so I was silent, giving her the opportunity to answer for me. "I presume you mean it will be difficult for you. Well every day is difficult for Ben. Every single day, every single moment. Perhaps I could impose on you to face some difficulty for forty-five minutes out of your day?" And with that, she handed me documents that outlined Ben's exact needs and gave me a time to meet with the team of folks who were in place to help Ben have a successful year. And, then, thankfully, she left.

Ben and I stumbled through the year. I got better at remembering early to give the one teacher's assistant we had for the entire seventh grade the texts that we'd be reading the next week, so she could get them copied and enlarged. I spent weekends retyping mimeographed worksheets that we'd be using the following week. I finally figured out that when I was going to transcribe what students were saying during discussions onto a blank transparency, I could appoint a scribe for Ben who would copy what I was writing on large sheets of paper with a fat-tipped marker. Ben got better at speaking up when I would write something on the blackboard that I hadn't already written out for him. ("Large font, black ink, remember?" he'd ask. "Right," I'd say, frustrated at having forgotten once again.) But we got through the year and on the last day of class, when he signed my yearbook in that large loopy scrawl of his, I knew I did not deserve the thanks he offered: "Thanks for being my teacher. You did a good job and I learned a lot. Ben. PS: You did a good job of helping me. Thank you." Ben might have been the student with the disability, but he was the one who taught me about possibility. He was the one who first showed me the true power of an inclusive classroom.

* * *

Ben had become a memory along with Mike, who had Tourette's Syndrome; Jeff, with deafness; Megan, who had cerebral palsy; and Kim, an undergraduate student who sat in my office one day crying because she was not going to be able to pass her college algebra course and no one at the university seemed to care about the documented learning differences she had in math. But this book brought them all back, because this book is not only about how we teach students with disabilities, it's about how we see past the disability to the heart of the student, to the possibilities inherent in that student. As I started to read this book, I looked at the title and presumed that the "power of inclusive classrooms" that the subtitle references was intended for students with disabilities. But this book quickly makes clear that the power of inclusion is as much for us, teachers, as it is for the student.

It was apparent to me that Patrick understands something we all need to understand. From the first pages of *From Disability to Possibility,* Patrick takes us into the lives of students with disabilities and reminds us all of the possibilities of inclusion—not just for students with special education needs, but for ourselves as well. He provides the concrete, specific information we need to make inclusion doable, and he provides the inspiration we need to make it desirable. He tells us the stories of what happens to kids when inclusion is truly inclusive, and he gives us the tips that make inclusion nonintrusive. He makes me—and he will, I anticipate, make you—rethink, in fact *revision,* the students with disabilities who come haltingly into our classrooms.

As I read this book, I thought often of my new favorite quote: "If you change the way you look at things, the things you look at change." This has become my mantra in the past few months. I say it when I look at my fifteen-year-old son's bedroom; I say it when I look at his haircut (or lack of); I say it when I step inside a classroom and see twenty-eight adolescents who don't want to be in sixth period remedial reading class. And, I said it over and over again as I read this book.

From Disability to Possibility will change the way you look at your students with disabilities. And when you make that shift, the way those students look to you *will* change. You will see the possibilities and in that vision, you *will* see the power of the inclusive classroom.

Kylene Beers, Ed.D.
Senior Reading Researcher
School Development Program
Yale University

Acknowledgments

As an adult with Attention Deficit Hyperactivity Disorder (ADHD), sitting down long enough to write a book was not exactly easy for me. Luckily, I had the following people to guide me powerfully, both in my education and in my writing.

Sandy Hilmert: No one would be holding this book now if it were not for you. Your unbelievable knack for connecting people brought me to the gurus and forum for progressive education: Smokey Daniels, Marilyn Bizar, and Walloon. Thanks also for your editing help and common sense. Your humor keeps me going amidst bureaucracy, outdated attitudes, darkness, and the word *"No!"*

Smokey Daniels: As the editor of this work, it is you who has made this whole process so affirming, educational, thought-provoking, and fun. You have been such a significant change agent for me—way more than you could ever comprehend. I respect you so much that as a result of our association, writing just comes out of me. Your person-centered abilities and beliefs are boundless. Thank you also for teaching me about literature circles, Hemingway, Walloon Lake, cowboy boots, and how to marry right. Here's to our continued association!

Leigh Peake: I will never ever forget the meetings we had after I gave my first speech at the Walloon Institute, or walking with you through Millennium Park. You know how to make a guy feel so upbeat about the way he maneuvers a keynote using plain talk, and you gave me a belief that there was a valuable book here in the midst of all my storytelling. You are brilliant in your perspective and wisdom.

Lynne Costa: As my Production Editor, you have healed me from the "red pen" experiences of my former days and have added collaboration, empowerment, and inspiration to the mix. You are phenomenal at what you do and a true team player.

Paula Kluth: You are so full of life, progressiveness, and energy, and you always have your foot in the next out-of-the-box realm of thinking. It is beyond comprehension that you have now become my neighbor! Good things do happen in life. Any room that has you in it becomes a better place by your mere presence. It is an honor to work with you and attend our monthly writing meetings. Salute!

Alice Udvari-Solner: In my career you are the leading lady who instilled a work ethic with backbone and the commitment to *just doing things right!* You are brilliant beyond belief, supportive, authentic, and the best darn first cooperating teacher a guy could ever wish and hope for. You most certainly taught me so much about HOW to teach!

Jacque Thousand and Richard Villa: I am in awe of you both. I will never forget shaking when I read the first writings of yours that I got my hands on. You were not only able to clearly and concisely articulate an educational model for many things I had been thinking about and feeling, you did it in an eloquent and humane way. Jacque, thank you also for your supportive editorial feedback and wonderful ideas, which greatly strengthened this book. I bow to you both.

Lou Brown and Anne Donnellan: Thank you so many times over for the hardcore education you provided me during the progressive days of special education. Both of you were significant change agents for our field and you modeled exactly what I needed to do to carry on your significant legacy. There is much change that still needs to happen and I thank you for keeping me strong and moving forward on the journey.

My teachers: Betsy Shiraga, Alison Ford, Pat Rogan, Jennifer Barr York, Jan Nisbet, Pat Mirenda, Mark Sweet, Kim Kessler, and Rick Mesaros: The astounding education you all provided me has shaped me as a teacher, professor, leader, and human being. The fact that you are all now leaders, shows the education world at its very best.

Jeanne Marquis and Mary Graczyk: After Alice, you became my next cooperating teachers. Thank you for confirming to me that out-of-the-box is good! Kindred spirits are hard to find these days, so I really lucked out with you two.

Tracy Lyndon: Way back when, you told me over lunch that I must write a book. Here it is and thank you so much for your inspiration, help, and support. Now it is *your* turn to write your book—I will call you for lunch!

People I work with day-to-day: Paul, Peggy, Alison, Jerry, Richard, Cheryl, Greg, Kathy, Howard, and all my National-Louis University and United Cerebral Palsy Infinitec Colleagues: How did I get so fortunate as to work with all of you? Thanks to everyone for continually teaching this teacher.

All the faculty and educators from the Walloon Institute: It has been such an honor to work with you all during the past two years. You have taken me to a new place in my educational beliefs and no group does the fun factor better!

Supportive friends: Boo, Buck, Raul, and Kassira: Thank you all for listening and hearing me out during all the adventures of this process, morning, noon, night, and midnight!

Tanita: Through your singing, you put me in the frame of mind to think, create, and write. No one else in the world has ever been able to do that for me, so thanks for being you!

And Very Importantly:

Thank you to all the individuals and family members whose stories make up this book! You have truly been my educators and I will never forget that I am working for you.

Much appreciation to all the school districts and agencies that I am honored to work with. You all know how to make a person who is on the fringes of things feel good about being that way!

I am forever indebted to all of the national and international places in the world who hire me to present, consult, and provide technical assistance. I do my best writing on an airplane, so thanks also to the many airlines, for keeping me from being distracted during the writing process. My second best place for writing is coffee houses, so thanks to all I have used for the java and the great writing environments!

And of course my family: *Vicky, Tim, Ma, Sarah, Bob, Katie, Haley, Welly and Chloe.* You make all of this worth it. I am fortunate. Life is good.

Introduction

Not long ago I was walking with my three-year-old niece Haley near her home. A man in a wheelchair passed by us, and Haley clung to my leg in fear. I was surprised, to say the least. I have dedicated my whole career to the field of special education, yet my own flesh and blood was scared of a person with a disability! What should I do?

Since I've been a public school and college teacher for fifteen years, the obvious solution presented itself. The natural way to address this predicament was to educate Haley. Prejudice is learned, and the way to combat it is through education and experience. But just talking to Haley would not be enough. I needed to find educational materials meaningful to a three-year-old. Perusing teacher stores and toy stores, I found "Becky," a Mattel doll who uses a wheelchair for mobility. I like Becky, because she has a cool red wheelchair, red sunglasses, and red hi-top sneakers. The box she comes in proclaims, "I am the school photographer," and displays pictures of Becky with lots of ambulatory friends from a variety of cultures.

(I did wonder why Becky wasn't just Barbie in a wheelchair. Why did she have a different name? Why couldn't a real Barbie have a physical challenge or a disability? But Barbie is all about *perfection*: young girls are taught these unrealizable expectations at a very early age. The body proportions of a Barbie doll are not achievable in real human beings except by extreme plastic surgery. Promoting such an unrealistic body image certainly holds psychological impact for girls and women of all ages!)

When I gave Haley the Becky doll, she opened the box, took Becky out, removed her from the wheelchair, and immediately undressed her (which I thought was pretty normal, since all her

Barbie dolls are typically naked and in a pile in her bedroom). Haley was treating Becky just the same as her other dolls. Next, she put naked Becky back in the wheelchair and asked me if I would play with her. We soon discovered that the wheelchair did not fit through the door of the Barbie Dream House and certainly did not fit into the Barbie Pink Corvette. Also, since the two-story dream house didn't have an elevator, the doll had to become "naked Becky in a flying wheelchair" in order to get to the upper floor!

> The inaccessibility Haley and I experienced in Barbieworld is the reality people with disabilities face every day.

The inaccessibility Haley and I experienced in Barbieworld is the reality people with disabilities face every day. Haley and I talked about these obstacles, and we also put an actual Barbie in the wheelchair. Next, wanting to introduce Haley to what I call person-first language, I taught her to say *people with disabilities* rather than *disabled people*. She had a hard time pronouncing the word *disabilities*—it kept coming out *possibilities*. Laughing, I told Haley I liked her word much better. My three-year-old niece had inspired me to reimagine special education in the United States as *possibility studies*.

Let's Get Special Education Right

Thirty years ago, special education as we know it today barely existed. It was a smattering of uncoordinated, hard-to-find, disparate programs mainly serving students with significant physical and cognitive challenges. The most common disabilities we now encounter in schools (learning disabilities, attention deficit disorder) were just being described and barely addressed. Today, there has been a revolution of recognition, legislation, and advocacy. Millions of students are now receiving special education assistance. Billions of dollars are spent each year for special education services.

But the huge institution that has grown up in connection with special education over the past few decades has been badly designed. The field is troubled, confused, struggling, and not producing acceptable results. Basic legislation designed to protect the rights of kids is often ignored or circumvented. An outdated but still prevalent medical and behavioral model deprives students of fair, effective, and personally empowering school experiences. We are trapped in a kid-unfriendly orthodoxy. The current state of affairs for students with disabilities in our schools is this:

> **A**n outdated but still prevalent medical and behavioral model deprives students of fair, effective, and personally empowering school experiences. We are trapped in a kid-unfriendly orthodoxy.

- There are millions of students with disabilities in the general education classroom. Many of these students with specialized learning needs simply go unserved by special educators. Just as worrisome, only one quarter of classroom teachers or general educators say that they feel prepared to serve these young people. The training, preparation, philosophical base, techniques, and strategies are not there to serve students effectively.
- The 78.3 billion dollars spent in America on special education at the local, state, and federal levels accounts for 21.4 percent of the 360.2 billion dollars spent annually on elementary and secondary education (American Institutes for Research 2004). Yet when we look at the ultimate outcomes, over 75 percent of public school graduates with disabilities are unemployed.
- The number of students identified as having learning disabilities grew 242 percent between 1979 and 1997 (American Institutes for Research 2004).
- The federal No Child Left Behind act requires that schools disaggregate test score data for students with special education needs. Often, these students have the lowest annual gains and, as a result, are blamed and stigmatized for low school performance.
- Most special education programs are not following the laws that established them.
- In too many cases, special education services simply do not work by any meaningful definition of the term. There are lower grades, lack of academic progress, more dropouts, alienation created by segregation, and stigmatization of students by adults with little or no background with educating diverse learners.

- American society includes a significant number of capable people with disabilities who wish to work but remain unemployed. As noted, 75 percent of people with disabilities who graduate from the public school system (a system that ostensibly prepares students for a successful life, to include employment) cannot find jobs (Walker 2004). And this unemployment rate continues to increase.
- Many people with disabilities who have been educated in our public school systems are not only unemployed but have empty social lives and remain living at home with their families until their parents die (Roessler 2002).

Three decades after the landmark special education legislation that held so much promise, special education is still just that—*a promise*. Our American school system and society have earned a failing grade for educating and supporting people with disabilities to live, work, and play in the community.

The good news is, there *is* a path forward and a way out. But we must adopt a whole new model, a new paradigm—one that grows out of contemporary cognitive science, not the discredited, blame-the-victim behaviorism of the 1950s. We need to honor the learning opportunities that students with diverse educational needs bring forward, not just label, berate, and isolate them.

This book introduces the specific kinds of teaching, classroom practices, and management approaches that bring this new model to life. It also explores the broader implications for providing better postschool outcomes for individuals with disabilities and their nondisabled counterparts. Specifically:

- This book is for classroom teachers and the special educators who partner with them. Really, it's for anyone who works with kids with disabilities, from the least intense learning challenges to the most significant, from preschoolers to adults.
- This book is mostly made up of stories about real kids and teachers and how they have struggled, solved problems, and succeeded.
- This book is practical. It shows how knowing teachers, parents, peers, and administrators are making special education services *work* for kids.

- This book is about *thinking* and *believing*. In those places where special services are especially effective, the adults have particular attitudes and strategies.

This book is about *thinking* and *believing*.

The current field of "disability studies" tells the stories of individuals with disabilities in their own, authentic voices: "I am a learning disabled person. I own this label, and I have something to say regarding what I liked and did not like about the educational system!" My own *possibility studies*, like disability studies, uses the life stories of people with disabilities to inform the field. But rather than emphasize a critical approach, I search, examine, and review these personal life stories for attributes and possibilities that can be used to plan and work toward outcomes that improve the quality of life at school, at home, and in the community.

These personal stories have led me to some ah-ha's; some conclusions that have become guiding principles for me have turned into tenets of my possibility studies. I share them with you here.

1. Diversity is good.
2. Special education is a service, not a sentence.
3. No double standards.
4. A general education shouldn't need to be earned.
5. Inclusion may not be easier, but it's better.
6. The dignity of risk applies to all people.
7. Parents are the gold standard.
8. Get rid of labels.
9. Make education real.
10. Disability is normal.

These tenets form the structure for this book as each becomes a chapter and each is illustrated with the student stories that show us how disabilities are best viewed as possibilities. You'll discover the stories to be thinking points; and somewhere on this journey you will find your own tenets that will help you create the inclusive classroom that indeed does turn disability into possibility.

And speaking of that classroom, if you're the kind of teacher I'm thinking about, you probably have a classroom of between twenty and thirty kids or a series of departmentalized classes. Within that student population is an increasing percentage of kids with diverse needs, with identified learning issues, whom you must educate along with everyone else. You may have quite a bit of assistance (paraeducators, special education coteachers, specially adapted materials and equipment) or may feel pretty much alone with few resources to help you. Whatever support you do have, you probably don't feel prepared to serve kids with LD, ADHD, BD, ED, or a dozen other labels. And you're right to feel ill-equipped: most of you have taken a single special education survey course in your teacher certification program. How could that have prepared you enough to address effectively the needs of the students in your classes? But though stretched thin, you're working hard and doing the best you can. Welcome, colleague, as we explore the possibilities of disabilities together.

Chapter **One**

Diversity Is Good

In science, there is a concept called biodiversity, which argues that an ecosystem with a wide and diverse array of life forms is healthier, stronger, and more enduring. Seen in this way, differences (the more, the better) are the building blocks of a robust, living community. The same principle applies to people in social groups, like neighborhoods, workplaces, and schools. Working with an unusually diverse group of people on a job or project, you've probably found yourself thinking, "Wow! We are coming up with so many great ideas. This is more effective (and more fun) than when everyone is just the same." What a dull place our world would be if everyone were exactly alike!

> **W**hat a dull place our world would be if everyone were exactly alike!

It is never too early or too late to start educating children about diversity. If children encounter diversity early on, it is easy for them to be natural around people who may walk, talk, or look different, or face hidden challenges such as learning disabilities or dyslexia. Children learn from people who are different from them. Let me state that even more strongly: children *need* to learn from people who are different from them, especially in light of the increasing cultural, social, and intellectual diversity in their own communities.

Cultural diversity is currently changing the landscape of many communities. Cultures that were once minorities are now becoming majorities. Take Chicago, where I live: Hispanics have now become the second-largest ethnic group in the city and will end up surpassing all other cultures in the Chicago area by 2050

(U.S. Census Office 2000). Chicago also has the second-largest Polish population in the world, after Warsaw (Wikipedia Encyclopedia 2005). Schools need to embrace the rich heritage and variety of cultures in their own communities. When they do, everyone benefits.

Family diversity is also changing the makeup of school communities. Variations in family structure have most certainly increased over the years: even the IRS now acknowledges *twelve* different types of families (Internal Revenue Service 2005). That is diverse! My second-grade teacher once asked how many of us had mothers who worked outside the home. Out of twenty-five students, only one raised his hand. These days, the ratio would probably be just the opposite.

Learning diversity has also grown or at least become better recognized. There have always been individuals who think in different ways, but since special education exploded with the passing of Public Law PL-94-142 in 1975, we have identified many new disabilities that affect learning. Today, schools spend great amounts of money, time, and effort identifying, labeling, and educating students. We need to change how we address learning diversity because of the hugely disappointing outcomes of special education. Reform is essential.

The first step in that reform is changing attitudes, helping people value diversity. Of course, diversity education is best delivered when students are very young. Nevertheless, education can move mountains at any age. Let's look at two examples.

Education can move mountains at any age.

Sam: Finding the Good in Everyone

Sam is a friendly and kind fifth grader with significant learning disabilities who lives next door to a public school. His sister Jessica is a year older than Sam and attends this neighborhood school. Since Sam has an identified learning disability and receives special education services, he is bused, forty-five minutes each way, to a school across town that serves students with learning disabilities. It seems very unfair that Sam has to get up much earlier in the morning and take a long bus ride when his sister can just walk next door five minutes before the bell rings.

When the school district instigates an inclusive education pilot program, Sam is chosen to receive special education services (including curricular adaptations, differentiated instruction, and speech/language instruction) in a general education classroom in his neighborhood school. At the beginning of each week, Sam's classroom teacher, the special education teacher, and the speech/language therapist go over the week's lessons and materials and decide how best to support Sam that week. (His parents are also encouraged to observe and participate.)

A social worker is also a very active presence in the school's classrooms. One day, in a lesson designed to build self-esteem, the social worker asks Sam and his classmates, individually, to brainstorm what things they do best and write down their ideas. Some of the students create a fairly lengthy list. When the social worker asks students to share their strengths with the class, many do so proudly. But when she asks Sam what he does best, he looks up, looks back down, and says, "N-n-n-nothing, there's nothing."

The social worker knows how to turn this difficult moment around: "Class, Sam is having a tough time coming up with what he does the best. What do you think he does the best?" The students come up with the following list:

- Smiling.
- Making friends.
- Being a good listener.
- Speaking up for himself.
- Being brave enough to come to a new school.
- Thinking things over when he makes a mistake.
- Being patient.
- Being courteous and following class rules.

Sam perks up as these ideas are shared. All in all, Sam's classroom colleagues are "pretty good kids" for noticing the positive qualities of a new student in the classroom, someone who appears the same as everyone else but learns differently. They have learned important lessons about finding the good in everyone and will benefit from this experience in future classrooms and in their adult lives. Furthermore, Sam is getting a much better education, closer to home.

Andrew: Going Places by Being Diverse

Andrew, a wise and insightful gentleman in his forties, has cerebral palsy. He went to a segregated school specifically for students with physical disabilities. I first met Andrew when he was attending a "training program" for adults with cerebral palsy and cognitive challenges (another version of a segregated school—as Lou Brown, a wise professor I once worked with, wrote, "Segregation begets segregation" [Brown et al. 1991]). I had been hired by the "training program" to help people live, work, and play within the community and had a little office in the building. One day Andrew appeared at the door. He tried to communicate with me, but I could not understand his vocalizations. To be fair to Andrew and honor him, I said, "Andrew, I see that you have something very important to tell me, and I know that other people around here understand you, even though I can't. Is there another way you can share this with me, so I can understand?"

Andrew motioned with his head toward the back of his wheelchair. I said, "Do you want me to help you get something out of your bag?" He nodded an energetic, "Yes!" I got the bag from the tray on the back of his wheelchair, and we pulled out a worn letter board. Andrew's pinky finger shot out to a series of letters on the board, spelling out a perfect, "Thank you." I knew then that Andrew was literate and had plenty to say, although it took a long time for him to communicate his thoughts to me by spelling out each word with his finger.

Andrew told me that he was married, and alluded to his segregated schooling. He also said that transportation was a big albatross for him, because he only received one round trip ride per day on a wheelchair-accessible van that was operated by the city transit authority. He and his wife enjoyed going out to restaurants and cultural events but had very limited opportunities to do so. Finally, Andrew confided that he wanted to be doing something other with his life than going to the "training program" for people with disabilities every day.

I told Andrew that there was technology available by which he could readily communicate his thoughts to people. I asked him if he would like me to help explore and address his communication needs. He nodded another vigorous yes. In conjunction with a speech specialist, we made an appointment with a Chicago Assistive Technology Center that would evaluate, make recommendations, and help Andrew secure the necessary technology. Andrew was the first person I knew who qualified for a DynaVox®, a device similar to a laptop computer that mechanically voices (there are a variety of choices: male, female, adult, child) whatever the user types in, allowing him or her to have reciprocal conversations. The keyboard can be customized to include pictures, words, and word phrases specific to the individual. Andrew's literacy and excellent spelling skills helped him immensely here.

Since Andrew was now equipped with a "voice," I asked him what he wanted to be doing in his life. He said that he wanted to work with children so that what had happened to him would not happen to anyone else. He wanted to educate people about disability.

We started to consider possibilities, brainstorm ideas, and pursue connections. One promising connection was a Montessori preschool for children ages two through six that was just down the block from the "training program" building. A neighborhood business alliance meeting that I attended was held in the preschool, and after the meeting, I approached the school's director. I told her there was a gentleman named Andrew who wanted to work with children. Would she and her colleagues be willing to let him visit and explore his dream job? The director was very accommodating: "Bring him in!" We set up a date.

When Andrew, mobile in his power wheelchair and able to communicate by means of his DynaVox, made his first visit, children swarmed around him asking, "Do you walk? Do you talk?" Mesmerized by his computer "voice," many children wanted to stay with Andrew during the remainder of the day. Andrew was a star! At the end of the visit, the director asked him please to return, and Andrew happily complied the following week.

After the second visit, the director asked Andrew if he could program some books for children into his DynaVox and read stories to the children the following week. Andrew immediately said yes. I panicked, because I had no clue how to help Andrew use the DynaVox for this new purpose. But we contacted a specialist to teach him how to program his DynaVox to "read" stories, and Andrew learned quickly. He was very thoughtful about it, also programming in instructions about when to turn the page, so a child could hold up the book and show the pictures as Andrew was reading.

Andrew was a big hit as a storyteller. He was immediately asked back to read more stories, and a week later the director asked him if he would like to work as a teaching assistant. Andrew had his first job, at forty-something, doing exactly what he wanted to do.

What I haven't told you yet is that the students in the Montessori preschool were being immersed in Spanish and Japanese. Andrew, a man who communicated using a mechanical voice, was a teaching assistant in a foreign-language Montessori preschool! I couldn't have been more delighted.

In my office, I have a photograph of Andrew reading to the children. I savor the fact that he is working at his first job. But I am equally excited for the children that now have Andrew for their teacher. It will be no big deal for these children to value someone with Andrew's attributes, someone who may get around using a wheelchair and communicate differently. I am excited by the thought of these future adults and their deeper understanding of diversity.

Sam's and Andrew's stories notwithstanding, I am scared by the reactions the general public has to disability and the field of special education. When I tell people that I am a special educator, they often say things like:

- "You must be so patient."
- "It takes a special person to do what you do."
- "I couldn't do that."
- "You're a saint before your time."

My typical response is, "You just have to like people." I do truly believe patience is a virtue, but it's not the most important attribute for a special educator. I am a man with ADHD, and patience does not come easy, nor is it always needed with my students. As for sainthood, I now have a T-shirt that proclaims, "Patrick was a saint, but I ain't!" Benevolence and pity drive most people with disabilities wild.

Fearful, benevolent, or pitying comments about disabilities reveal a lack of education and experience. People who make these kinds of remarks did not have people with disabilities in their classrooms or neighborhoods. Young people who don't interact with people who have "possibilities" can become thoughtless, condescending adults. There are generations of these individuals walking around out there in the world.

In the past, people with disabilities lived segregated lives, often shamed, silenced, and rendered invisible by their nondisabled counterparts. Not having respectful, meaningful, direct experiences with people who have disabilities fosters prejudice among the general public. We need to undo this prejudicial lack of education and experience by including individuals with disabilities in all walks of life, from womb to tomb. We need people with disabilities in our neighborhoods and communities, in our workplaces, stores, restaurants, and movie theaters. And an inclusive school community is the place to start.

The well-being of people with disabilities is in the hands of the general public. I know many adults with disabilities who are unemployed. I promise you, if you approached each of them right now, every one of them would say he or she wants to be employed. And most unemployed individuals with disabilities have had some kind of vocational training; they are qualified to work. People with disabilities are unable to get into the workplace because of the attitudes of the general public about disability! However innocently, nondisabled people have created very dismal futures for individuals with disabilities. If nondisabled people do not grow up alongside and receive an education with people who have disabilities, the likelihood of creating responsive citizens who understand diversity is greatly diminished.

When inclusion in schools is undertaken conscientiously and supportively, our communities improve. I recently met Barry, a young gentleman whose family put up quite a fight to see that he was included in the public schools of their community—in fact, they had to move to a different community to make it happen. He has now graduated from high school and is employed in two jobs. In his grocery store job, his boss is one of his former classmates, who knows Barry from school and likes and encourages him.

One of the most important reasons we need to educate our youth about diversity early (remembering too that it is never too late) relates to our own future. Someday, we will all have a disability, if we are lucky enough to get it—it is called old age. Many things we currently take for granted, we won't be able to do. But we will be happy to be a senior citizen with a full life of family and friends. Young people educated about diversity become more understanding, supportive, and responsible citizens and will create a better future world for us when we are seniors with a disability!

Chapter **Two**

Special Education Is a Service, Not a Sentence!

Whenever I teach a class of university students who are preparing to become special education teachers, I begin by asking them to tell me what they hope to be doing in five years. Many reply, "I would like to be teaching in a self-contained class-room." Then I also ask, "What is the legal purpose of special education?" I typically hear everything but the right answer, which is: *Special education is a service, not a place, and the purpose of the service is to support learners in successfully achieving a general education.* Many of my students seem puzzled by this answer, if not shocked. The reason for this reaction is the paradigm that has been perpetuated as a result of an incorrect interpretation of the Individuals with Disabilities Education Act (IDEA).

> **S**pecial education is a service, not a place, and the purpose of the service is to support learners in successfully achieving a general education.

The landmark IDEA was originally Public Law 94–142, enacted in 1975, with reauthorizations through the present. The original IDEA:

- Contained a "zero reject" clause: it guaranteed a free appropriate public education for all students with disabilities who qualify for services, ages 3–21.
- Authorized special education and related services to meet these students' unique needs.
- Protected the rights of children with disabilities and their parents.

- Required that testing and evaluation materials and procedures used to identify and place children with disabilities not be culturally or racially discriminatory.
- Called for individualized education programs (IEPs).
- Mandated a least-restrictive environment. Children with disabilities must *to the maximum extent appropriate* be educated with children who do not have disabilities; children with disabilities may be removed from the general education environment and taught separately only when the nature or severity of the disability is such that education in regular classes cannot be achieved satisfactorily even with the use of supplementary aids and services.
- Required appropriate instructional placement within a continuum of services ranging from the most to least segregated educational settings.
- Stipulated that information about programs, resources, and services must be made available to children with disabilities and their parents.
- Instituted a system of checks and balances to ensure accountability and fairness for students with disabilities and their families, including parental permission for evaluation, services, and placement; independent review and evaluation; hearings and appeals; and confidentiality.
- Authorized federal funding.

The most recent changes, in 2004, provide greater access to the general education classroom via assistive technology, require more highly qualified special education teachers, and reduce the paperwork related to and the amount of detail required in the IEP. The burden of proof is now on families rather than school districts to demonstrate whether the "free" education is not appropriate in a due process scenario. This is a massive shift of focus and truly scary for families.

The 1975 interpretation of this law was to put small numbers of students with "like" special education needs in self-contained classrooms so they could receive individualized attention. However, follow-up studies have shown that because of this segregation, general educators never became professionally prepared to educate the range of diverse learners who could and should be learning in the least-restrictive environment—that is, the general education classroom. These studies also showed that students with disabilities were unemployed after high school, went on living with their parents, and had few if any social relationships. Segregation was being promoted from childhood to adulthood.

The same lack of success is with us today, and we need to change our special education practices. Let's meet two students with diverse educational needs whose stories teach us the importance of creating plans to support them in general, not segregated, classrooms.

Susan: Making Difference Ordinary

New fifth-grader Susan is physically gifted. As adherents of Howard Gardner's multiple intelligence theory might say, she has a strong bodily-kinesthetic intelligence. Susan can run fast, throw far, and jump high. She shines during physical education class and school intramurals. She is well respected by students and adults alike for her physical talents and skills. Susan also has significant learning disabilities, especially in visually processing written language and in comprehending written material. From first through fourth grade, Susan has been educated in a self-contained classroom for students with learning disabilities in her local school district.

Susan's school district has now begun to reorganize their services for students with learning disabilities and has decided to eliminate the self-contained classroom and provide special education support in their general classrooms. Susan will now have a special educator, Paola, who will help Susan's classroom teacher, Barb, plan and provide curricular adaptations and differentiated instruction opportunities for Susan and other diverse learners. Susan will also have some direct support and study time with Paola each day.

In her new classroom, Susan has become acquainted with lots of students she didn't know before. In general, the year has started out well, and she has developed new social relationships in physical education class, on the playground, and in school intramurals. Her physical gifts are serving her well.

Susan's presence in the general education classroom requires the team responsible for her education to do business in a new way. Special educator Paola now serves students in many class-rooms, not just one, and must plan and coteach with these addi-tional classroom teachers, which requires new skills and a height-ened level of collaboration. Susan's classroom teacher, Barb, now has greater learning diversity in her classroom—not only Susan, but other students with diverse educational needs as well. Barb is the expert on fifth-grade curriculum; Paola is the expert on learn-ing individualization. Barb and Paola meet each week, go over Barb's upcoming lessons and materials, and decide what supports Susan and the other diverse learners' need. Paola then gives ideas for differentiation of the curriculum and arranges individualized support as necessary. They keep a detailed planning book that captures their decisions and efforts.

One learning support they implement for Susan is to use what they term *prelessons* in connection with language arts. Before any language arts lesson, Paola or Susan's speech and language spe-cialist, Pat, spends a few minutes with her going over key vocabu-lary words and reading passages. Susan also receives comprehen-sion questions in advance, so she is prepared to contribute to classroom discussions. And any passage Susan will be asked to read aloud in class is assigned the day before so that she can prac-tice it for homework. Reading out loud on the spot is very difficult for Susan and fraught with potential embarrassment. However, when she has the chance to prepare and practice her oral reading in advance, she can do it successfully. (Only her teachers and her parents know about these advance reading assignments.)

Another language arts support is an additional exposure to each story, perhaps reading it with a peer or listening to a recording of someone reading it. (Parent volunteers have recorded books for which commercial recordings are not available.) Barb is also using innovative differentiated instruction strategies like cooperative learning, peer mentors, and literature circles (Daniels and Steineke 2004), which help Susan be more successful in language arts.

Embedded cross-subject strategies help Susan learn in all sub-ject areas. Susan has difficulty taking complete notes, so she often doesn't have all the material she needs when she is studying for tests and other assessments. Realizing that a number of other learners in the class also struggle with taking notes, Barb appoints a "note taker of the day," chosen from a pool of students who take notes well. The note taker of the day posts or e-mails his or her notes for other students to consult.

Susan also struggles to read any text because of her visual processing difficulties. Her team comes up with three strategies to help her. The first is to highlight text before she reads it (Barb, Paola, and the classroom paraeducator all pitch in). Susan can then read just the highlighted main points. One day, one of Susan's classmates wonders out loud, "Why does she get that highlighted text; is she dumb?" A moment like this could have really hurt Susan's self-esteem, but Barb doesn't skip a beat: "University students highlight their texts to help them learn better, and highlighting also helps Susan learn better. We all need to learn how to do it." The next day she gives everyone a photocopy of the next chapter and teaches the class techniques related to highlighting text. Barb has not only made difference ordinary, she's given it prestige.

The second strategy is to insert sticky-note bookmarks into Susan's texts that adapt and summarize what is being said and alert her to what she is responsible for knowing.

On average, she needs twice as much time to complete assignments as a typical student. Susan's teachers don't want her education to feel like a punishment.

The final strategy is to reduce the amount of Susan's class work and homework. On average, she needs twice as much time to complete assignments as a typical student. Susan's teachers don't want her education to feel like a punishment.

Gavin: Creating a Support Plan around a Student Without Prerequisites

Gavin, energetic and spry, has quite different learning needs from Susan—he has autism as an attribute. He was in first grade at the time of this story. The year before, he had been placed in a self-contained classroom for students with autism and—a catch-all term—"pervasive developmental challenges." But during that year his family decided that they would move into a new school district, a fully inclusive one for which I was a consultant. I visited Gavin in his self-contained classroom, bringing along the principal and the special education director with whom I worked. The day we visited, Gavin was running and bouncing around the classroom, making noise, carrying a big Tinkertoy® stick, and receiving goldfish cracker reinforcements every few minutes. I wondered what his teachers were trying to reinforce.

At different points during that day both the principal and special education director asked me, "Patrick, can we include this one?" I said, "Yes" (without a plan), but added, "We'll need to build a careful set of supports around his individual educational needs." I also realized that the layout of Gavin's new school would be quite different from the current one. The classroom we were observing in had four walls and a door. His new school didn't have walls between classrooms; bookshelves and cabinets loosely defined the grade-level boundaries as an open environment. One could see the whole school (primary and intermediate grades) from any point in the large room.

When Gavin arrived at his new school the following year, he wanted to engage in the activities he'd "learned" in his previous school—running around, making noise, and seeking food—which he proceeded to do as the teachers shot daggers at me. (If looks could kill!)

I addressed an emergency faculty meeting at the end of the day. I started out by saying, "I realize you have all met Gavin today." The faculty nodded, arms crossed, furious looks on their faces. "You no doubt think Gavin is a student with behavior issues." Heads nodded even more vigorously. "There is something that you all need to know about Gavin. He has autism, and something we know about people with autism is that they can handle only a little change at a time. Gavin has a brand new home and also a new school. I don't see him as a student with behavior issues, I see him as a scared little boy." The faces of my audience began to soften. "We need to make some changes to help Gavin acclimate to the school. Starting tomorrow, Gavin will be delivering your mail to you, and if you need to send any mail to the school office, he will also provide that service." (By designating Gavin as school courier, I made it okay for him to be in every room of the school—we had to start somewhere.) "Also, during each class period, he will be expected to do some work related to what is being taught in his general education classroom."

The school's team of educators met with Gavin's mom in order to understand more deeply the best ways and means to support Gavin. During the meeting, his mom asked where the net swing was going to be placed. (A net swing provides rhythmic motion that helps learners with Gavin's needs handle their day better. Use of such supports is termed *sensory integration*. [Kluth 2003]) General education classrooms don't have net swings, so I asked the school's occupational therapist, who was at the meeting, "Carla, are there any other means to achieve this that work well in a general education classroom?" Carla suggested a rocking chair, and after the meeting I went to a local department store and purchased two little rocking chairs for the classroom. That way other students would be able to use one as well (another way to make difference ordinary). I initially put both rocking chairs in the reading area, and later moved one next to Gavin's desk so he could use it whenever he wanted. Since Gavin arrived at school early, I also made sure he got in a good session on the playground swings before school started. And at recess, Gavin was always the first one on the swings.

Carla introduced some additional sensory integration experiences that helped Gavin feel more internally organized and learn more effectively. She had a little stiff-bristled brush that she stroked along his arms. When several students in the classroom asked if they could help "brush" Gavin, Carla agreed. Soon students began to fight over who got to brush Gavin, making him feel very popular.

When Gavin was completing his messenger rounds, he liked to lie down in between some tumbling mats outside the gym and have his paraeducator put pressure on the mats. (Dr. Temple Grandin, a brilliant animal science professor who also happens to be an adult with autism, designed something similar called a "squeeze-box.") However, when the other students saw this, they were worried: "We realize he runs around and makes noise in the school, but do they have to crush him in between those mats?" Obviously we needed to educate everyone in the school about autism, sensory integration, and what they could do as Gavin's classmates to best support him. Gavin's mother and Paula, his special education teacher, made presentations to each class.

Communication was also an essential goal for Gavin. For the most part, Gavin was nonverbal, but he made specific vocalizations to convey things only he knew. His teachers started to use pictures in connection with words, so Gavin could make choices and be more empowered, have more control over his environment.

Gradually, the number of stops on Gavin's mail run were reduced, thus decreasing the number of places it was acceptable for him to be. His teachers also increased the amount of time he spent engaging with the first-grade curriculum, adapting assignments and providing support as necessary. Eventually, Gavin was able to say particular words. He also became better at making his needs known, and his interfering actions (running around, making noise, seeking food) for the most part ceased.

Gavin's story is still very much in progress. However, he has lunched with the superintendent of the school district, and he walked (he didn't run) across the auditorium stage for his eighth-grade graduation. My fear is that if we had not started supporting the first-grade Gavin by understanding the communicative intent of his behavior and by meeting his sensory needs—if we had tried to make him sit in his desk all day—we would now have a much larger "kid" running around and making noise. With a support plan, his learning gains have been significant, and he is a testament to the success of inclusion.

> **W**ith a support plan, his learning gains have been significant, and he is a testament to the success of inclusion.

Fairness Is Not Sameness

Some may ask, why is all this time being spent helping one student? Is this fair to the others? Richard Lavoie (1998) replies, "Fair does not mean that each student gets the same thing, but each student gets what he or she needs." Putting these support strategies in place for Susan and Gavin provides individualization for them as learners and takes steps toward making the classroom more differentiated for all students. Learning in general improves as teachers use more of the tools and techniques in their bag of educational tricks. The gains of even one learner are worth the effort! Often, meeting the learning needs of students on either end of the learning spectrum (students with gifts and students with challenges) improves the quality of education in the entire classroom. Once these supports are in place, any lesson will support a greater range of learning needs.

Including students like Susan and Gavin in a general education classroom may not be easier, but it is better. Why shouldn't every student's first option be an age-appropriate general education classroom in their neighborhood school, supported by curricular adaptations and differentiated instruction?

Chapter **Three**

No Double Standards

I sometimes begin my workshops with an activity I call Name That Educator. We start out with two pieces of chart paper, one headed *What Is a General Educator?* and the other, *What Is a Special Educator?* Using sticky notes, the participants contribute as many characteristics to each chart as they can brainstorm. Then I put up a new piece of chart paper headed *What Is an Educator?* and ask them to move as many sticky notes as are appropriate from the other pieces of chart paper to this one. All of the sticky notes always end up on the new chart.

This simple exercise is eye-opening. Walls and double standards are erected when special and general educators are trained separately and differently. Traditionally, general educators contend, "I made a concerted effort to become a general educator; let's leave the education of kids with disabilities to the special educator." Traditionally, special educators believe, "I want a small, self-contained classroom in which I can individualize the curriculum for my students; it would be ridiculous for me to have to know the entire general school curriculum."

> **W**alls and double standards are erected when special and general educators are trained separately and differently.

But these traditional viewpoints are outdated now that general educators deal with much more diversity in their classrooms and special educators are responsible for helping their learners achieve a general education. All teachers are wearing a greater variety of hats and hold a greater variety of responsibilities. Today, neither general nor special educators have the luxury of saying who they will and will not educate, not to mention how they will do so. Since there is no one way to educate students, it is wrong to assert that a general educator doesn't need to know diverse learner strategies or that a special educator doesn't need to know the general curriculum. Education must become more multifaceted and dynamic if it is to work for everyone.

> Education must become more multifaceted and dynamic if it is to work for everyone.

I am not saying that our students do not need both general and special educators, only that training in both fields needs significant reform. We must abolish the we-they mentality that exists between them and consider the education of all students to be the responsibility of every teacher. In order to focus on best practice for all students, *all* educators need to be well versed in the following educational practices:

- Collaboration. Collaboration is not an option, it's a must. No one educator should shoulder the sole responsibility of adapting curriculum and methods for diverse learners. Everyone must contribute and take responsibility as a team.
- Openness to new ideas. Educators must seek creative and imaginative solutions to opportunities or issues surrounding the needs of diverse learners.
- Knowledge of curriculum. Educators must stay current through preparation, research, and investigation.
- Differentiated instruction. This planning, design, and teaching approach is a means to meet the needs of the entire range of learners in the classroom. As much as possible individual needs should be met *within lessons* rather than through individual adaptations.
- Distinct, equitable coteaching. Special educators should not be relegated to the role of paraeducator in the general classroom.
- Effective, ongoing planning.
- A zero rejection policy (Villa and Thousand 2001). No educator should draw the line between who will and will not learn in a classroom.

> Obviously, one introductory college course dealing with learners with disabilities is not nearly enough preparation for a general educator.

Obviously, one introductory college course dealing with learners with disabilities is not nearly enough preparation for a general educator.

A defining moment for me professionally was being hired as a professor at National-Louis University. During my interview, the dean handed me a copy of *Best Practice*, by Steven Zemelman, Harvey (Smokey) Daniels, and Art Hyde, who were about to become my colleagues. Perusing the book, I saw that many of their recommendations had to do with diverse learners and the coming together of general educators and special educators. Their principles of best-practice learning belonged on my list of practices for differentiated instruction for learners with diverse educational needs. As much as we may try to sort, label, and segregate learners, every classroom these days is a diverse entity: general and special education best practice must come together to meet the needs of all.

> **G**eneral and special education best practice must come together to meet the needs of all.

Let's look at some of the double standards we mistakenly create for and apply to students with and without disabilities.

Marco: Don't Hold a Disability Against a Person

Marco, a learner who very carefully watched what other students were doing in the school, was a student with an IEP and was first included in a general education classroom in fifth grade. He had some catching up to do with regard to literacy and in the other curricular areas and needed lots of support. It was a tough road, and the fatigue of meeting increased expectations showed often on his face. But his classroom supports were being examined and altered as needed.

During recess, Marco went to the playground with all the other fifth graders. One day, two girls reported that Marco had pulled down his pants. The next morning, the principal also received a phone call from one of the girl's parents. Knowing that Marco was a student with special needs, this parent offered her opinion that "perhaps Marco should be removed and put back into a self-contained classroom." The principal responded that Marco was most certainly not the first student in the school to engage in this type of behavior—she had quite a record of similar incidents, all by students without IEPs.

Investigating Marco's behavior on the playground, the principal made an interesting discovery. When she asked Marco and his mother where he might have learned this behavior, she discovered that Marco had attended one of his brother's football games recently. During the game, a male high school student had pulled down his pants, receiving quite a roar of approval from the rowdy crowd. Marco had learned his "antisocial" behavior from a student without a disability. The principal enjoyed relaying this information to the parent who had complained and telling her that Marco would be disciplined as any other student would be—and that removal from the classroom would most certainly not be one of the consequences.

Why did this parent bring up Marco's disability in the first place? The most likely reason is that she probably had not encountered people with disabilities during her own education. Without the knowledge (and education) that people with disabilities are more similar to nondisabled people than different, a double standard is easily created. Earlier segregationist practices mean that much work needs to be done to reeducate those who have prejudicial views about diversity.

> Without the knowledge (and education) that people with disabilities are more similar to nondisabled people than different, a double standard is easily created.

Although this principal had not received other complaints about students with IEPs in general education classrooms, she thought it might be a good idea for all parents in the school district to have a chance to learn the facts about inclusion. In conjunction with the district's special education director, she organized a community presentation on the topic. The principal and the special education director also made ongoing presentations on inclusion to the local school board. Education itself is the best way to do away with double standards and prejudices about learners with diverse educational needs.

Zach: Learning the Rules

Zach is a sixth grader with an eye for jokes and fun who was also previously in a self-contained classroom. At his IEP placement meeting when he entered middle school, the educational team decided that Zach would receive special education supports in a general education classroom. A general educator (Kathryn) and a special educator (Sheila) who cotaught in the middle school felt Zach was a perfect candidate for their classroom. (Oftentimes, placements for students with IEPs become more restrictive as they grow older, but Zach was lucky.)

In his elementary school, Zach would sometimes go into the girls' restroom. Because he was a student with diverse educational needs and was segregated in the self-contained classroom, the teachers and paraeducators pooh-poohed this behavior ("Come on now, Zach") and ignored it. No wonder Zach kept on doing it.

When Zach went into the girls' restroom at his new school, however, Kathryn and Sheila sent him to the principal's office, after discussing with the principal in advance what the consequence should be. Discovering that a typical male student would receive a detention in the principal's office for this offense, Sheila and Kathryn agreed that Zach should also receive a detention.

When the principal told Zach he would need to sit detention in his office (abbreviating the duration a little since it was his first offense), Zach cried a little, obviously scared, hurt, and upset. But afterward, he never went into the girls' restroom again. Learning had fortunately taken place. What if Zach had continued to be judged against a double standard? What if he had continued to enter women's restrooms as a high school student or as an adult. After all, it was a *learned* behavior.

Creating a double standard for students just because they have a special education label does not serve them well for learning real-life rules and expectations. Sometimes we think we are doing someone with an identified disability a favor by not giving them consequences for an interfering action; it is really no favor at all—we are doing the individual a disservice in learning and in life.

Dining in Siberia

The educational model in the school where I got my first teaching job was self-contained classrooms for students with special education needs, along with a lot of instruction outside school about how to live, work, and play in the community. Because so much instruction took place outside the school setting, the students with special education needs and their teachers were very isolated from the general education students and faculty. This isolation was particularly apparent during lunchtime: the students with special education needs would eat lunch in their self-contained classroom or sit in a segregated group in the cafeteria. As a new and eager special education teacher, I was going to change the world—or at least the high school cafeteria!

Having all the students with special education needs grouped at the same table emphasized their differences. And if they were not in the cafeteria at all, an important learning opportunity about diversity was being denied the entire student body who would someday become the adults of the community. I certainly did not want to stop students with possibilities from being friends with other students with diverse educational needs. However, in my role as an agent for change, I decided to make sure that all students ate lunch in the cafeteria and that the segregated lunch table was eliminated.

Achieving this "better cafeteria" required a significant amount of retraining for students both with and without disabilities. Staff and paraeducators also needed some training about why we should all be in the cafeteria and where we should be seated—that is, all over the place!

Once the students with special education needs were integrated throughout the cafeteria, however, I realized how subdued they were when they were eating. This may be what lunchroom supervisors dream about, but it created walls between students with and without disabilities. I worked on getting my students to loosen up and have more fun in the cafeteria, surreptitiously instigating a number of lively episodes in an effort to foster greater acceptance and understanding, to get the students to focus on their similarities rather than their differences. We initiated a topic-of-the-day discussion, so students with diverse education needs were initiating conversations about the football game, big news stories, movies and music. We ensured the topics were the hot items from the school or media.

The segregated lunch table is a double standard in many, many schools these days, one often encouraged by the faculty and administration. This needs to change. And we might also encourage our students to act more like typical adolescents in the cafeteria instead of perfect little angels.

Eric: Advocate for Students

Eric, a former high school student of mine, had a difficult life. He had been placed in a foster home because of the physical, emotional, and sexual abuse he had endured in his biological family. His efforts to cope were not always successful, and many of his interfering actions such as hitting took place at school.

Eric struggled with oral communication, and often, in frustration, he hit the students who upset him. The principal suspended him after each incident and threatened expulsion if the hitting continued. Realizing the likely inefficacy of this form of discipline, I investigated what Eric was communicating by hitting, that is, why he was acting this way. It seemed highly probable that Eric had learned to strike others from observing and experiencing his biological family's reaction to stress. Eric himself had been abused; in turn, he tried to abuse others.

I needed to do something to stop this abuse cycle before Eric was expelled. I increased the number of sessions he spent with his therapist and became his advocate when difficulties arose. I also realized he needed something meaningful to him. I knew he was awed and excited by anything having to do with firefighting. I also knew the high school had a work-study program for students both with and without disabilities. I asked the principal if I could explore an outside work-study placement for Eric at the local fire department.

While it may seem to some that I was employing a double standard by saving Eric from expulsion and pulling strings for him at the firehouse, Eric's situation as a student caught within a cycle of abuse definitely came first. If I did not act as an advocate and as an agent for change, Eric would be an expelled high school dropout without a future. Wasn't my job to help individuals with a variety of challenges to achieve a quality future? The choice seemed clear.

With the principal's very reluctant permission, I developed a work-study opportunity for Eric at the fire station. I won't ever forget taking him to the station to begin his job there. He hugged me in gratitude. He remained in this work-study position for the rest of high school, and the incidents of his fighting in the hall ceased. Eric also endeared himself to the firefighters and became a very popular daily presence.

In summary, then, first and foremost, it is essential not to create double standards for what initially seem like two worlds: general education and special education. These supposedly disparate worlds and students are much more alike than they are different. Once again, we need both specialties—general *and* special education—to meet the needs of all learners. What comes first with any and all students are successful learning outcomes and futures. If we can put the students—their stories, their needs—first, without creating outdated, destructive double standards, we will create a better future generation of citizens, people who empathize more deeply and understand the value and power of diversity. Diversity is our strength if we allow it to be so.

Diversity is our strength if we allow it to be so.

Chapter **Four**

A General Education Shouldn't Need to Be Earned

Anthony: The Least Restrictive Environment and System Reform

Anthony, tall and athletic, is a fifth grader with significant learning disabilities who attends a public school in a Chicago suburb. He is good-looking, sporting a popular style of haircut and fashionable clothes. Anthony is immediately likeable, and his social interactions are typically well received. Previously, Anthony had been a member of a self-contained classroom of students with learning disabilities and behavioral challenges, but he currently attends a general education fifth-grade classroom for most of his school day (he also spends some homework review and support time alone with his special education teacher, Sally). Anthony receives shorter language arts and mathematics homework assignments than his classmates, since it takes him approximately twice as long to complete them. This adaptation is delineated on his individual education plan.

Anthony is having trouble at home. His parents are separated, his father has moved out of the house, and divorce proceedings are in progress. His mother does not have enough money to keep the house, so she is going to put it on the market, and she and Anthony are going to move in with her parents. His father has been seeing Anthony less and less; the last time was two months ago. These changes have been hard on Anthony. He is more easily frustrated and has frequent outbursts at school and home. When Anthony's mom decides to seek work in California near her sister and leave

Anthony with her parents (so he won't have to change schools), his outbursts increase. He wants to be back with his parents in their old home. He feels that he has lost everything that is important to him.

One day Anthony comes to school so upset that he throws a desk directly at a teacher. Anthony's IEP team calls a special meeting, which Anthony's grandparents attend. The team feels that because of Anthony's difficult situation, he needs the support offered by therapy. They decide to send him to an alternative school that has a staff therapist, and to review his case in a month. Anthony has "earned" his way out of the general education classroom.

Overhaul the Continuum of Services!

America has created a system whereby learners with special education needs are, in many cases, identified, tested, labeled, and segregated before they ever have a chance to function in a general education environment. This practice violates the concept of *least restrictive environment* and misinterprets what *continuum of services* means. The continuum of services delineates placement options for students with identified special education needs from the least restrictive (the general education classroom) to the most restrictive (an outside segregated placement). Instead, *continuum of services* is often used as a scapegoat to deny learners from having general education opportunities. Because of this fact, the institutionalized view of the continuum of services needs overhauling. Look at Anthony. First, he began his education in a self-contained classroom and had to *earn his way into* a general education classroom, when he should have started out there in the first place (it is the least restrictive environment). Then, when behavioral problems arose, he was immediately put into an alternative school.

Are there times when a general education classroom does not serve a learner best and other options need to be explored? In Anthony's case, his frustration had reached dangerous levels: he posed a safety risk to himself and others. But does this mean we throw away the key to a general education classroom? Wait a minute!

If the purpose of special education is to provide the services that will garner learners with challenges a general education, a reintegration plan needs to be designed that will allow students who are receiving services in a self-contained classroom or some other alternative environment to return to their general education classroom. What factors and criteria determine when the return takes place? All too often, these questions are never asked. *But they need to be asked—they are integral to the intent of special education and the purpose of the law.* Many students with behavioral issues never return to the general education classroom: they've been handed a sentence, not provided a service. This practice needs to stop because it is not child-centered (that is, individualized) or educationally responsible.

> **M**any students with behavioral issues never return to the general education classroom: they've been handed a sentence, not provided a service. This practice needs to stop because it is not child-centered (that is, individualized) or educationally responsible.

Anthony's team decided the criteria for his return to his general education classroom would be these: he had to go one month without any explosions of temper and show that he accepted the reality that he needed to live with his grandparents. The team also agreed that Anthony would be able to continue receiving therapy after he returned to his general education classroom.

The General Education Curriculum Rules

In the meantime, while Anthony was receiving therapy at the alternative school, what should his education be like? This was a vital question. The first essential ingredient was a well-trained, sensitive teacher. In either an alternative placement or self-contained setting, such a teacher, first and foremost, matches the curriculum of the general education classroom. For Anthony's excellent teacher, this meant he needed to work with the same texts and materials being used in his general education fifth-grade classroom, as adapted to his literacy, understanding, and challenges. Only by keeping up with the same work as his classmates back in the general education classroom could Anthony be prepared to reintegrate once he met the criteria of the plan.

These adaptations were critical to Anthony's success. Without them, Anthony would not be guided toward a successful general education. Adapting the material used in the general education classroom is the job of any special educator, in whatever school, environment, or setting she or he practices. And differentiated instruction strategies used by general education teachers reduce the number of individual adaptations necessary, because the classroom lessons and materials already meet the needs of a greater range of learners.

Sometimes special educators who work in settings where the primary focus is teaching life skills feel they don't have to worry about the general education curriculum. Once again, wait a minute! Life skills are best taught and reinforced when and where they need to be used rather than by creating a separate, segregated life-skills program. Often, even life-skills programs set up in local neighborhood schools create a world of their own. The real world does not contain separate grocery stores, restaurants, and hotels for the general public and people with disabilities. Everyone lives in this world together, and they need to be educated together. (Chapter 9 focuses on making education real for all students.)

Are you curious as to what became of Anthony after he transferred to the alternative school? I am very glad to report a happy ending (but that's often not the case in similar situations). After six months, Anthony met the stipulated criteria of the reintegration plan—no explosions of temper for a month and a demonstrated acceptance of living with his grandparents—and returned to his general education fifth-grade classroom. Even though it was near the end of the school year, Anthony had used the same materials his former classmates were studying, so he was not behind (of course, he still needed curricular adaptations and differentiated instruction strategies). Anthony also continued to have therapy sessions outside school hours. The educators in both his neighborhood school and the alternative school had done their jobs! Anthony continued to improve; his own quality of life was better, and so was his grandparents'.

Jenny: A Free Appropriate Public Education Is Not Always Free or Appropriate

Not all tough diverse learner situations proceed as smoothly as Anthony's. Here's another case history. Jenny, an attractive and shy student with learning and literacy challenges, is about to begin high school. Except for kindergarten, Jenny has spent her elementary school years in a classroom for students with learning disabilities. She not only didn't begin her education in a general education classroom, she never had the opportunity to "earn" her way into one. An unwritten school district practice mandated that students with Jenny's learning needs be educated in a segregated setting. Period. Also, very illegal.

Furthermore, for too long, Jenny's individual education plan has remained static. Her goals, objectives, and benchmarks have stayed the same from year to year. In addition, her literacy skills have not developed as they might reasonably be expected to. In short, this approach to Jenny's education is not working, and her family wants a new one, one that will produce some positive results. And that's only natural. If a business doesn't grow from year to year, isn't a change of plan in order? Schools are not businesses, of course, but they are accountable for successful learning. (No matter the age of the student, he or she is still the most important thing in the world to his or her family. The best quality that educational professionals can bring to the table is empathy. Educational professionals who do for others what they would want done for their own children are doing their job.)

Jenny's family wants her to receive services and supports that will jump-start and spark her learning. They want her to be interested in and excited about school, and to that end they feel she needs to attend general education high school classes. They want her to experience the sights, sounds, and learning opportunities of a typical student and receive the proper special education and literacy support to do so successfully. Since they feel Jenny's literacy needs have not been addressed meaningfully over time, they request that her IEP also include the services of a reading specialist.

At a meeting with Jenny's family, school district representatives maintain that she cannot receive the services of a special education teacher and a reading specialist at the same time. This is a very blatant, very big red flag: the school district is admitting it is not willing to provide Jenny with all the individualized services she needs, which is the primary purpose of special education. Many students receive two or more primary and related services in order to succeed in school.

Not surprisingly, Jenny's family has now sought legal counsel, so that their daughter can receive an education in a meaningful, general setting with the proper related services that will allow her to learn, grow, and succeed. It is a tragic point at which to arrive. More stakeholders are added to the mix: lawyers for both Jenny's family and the school district become part of the decision-making team.

How much will the school district pay their lawyer so they do not have to provide special education and reading specialist services at the same time to a student who has not made progress for years and desperately needs both? How long will the school district remain entrenched in a nonindividualized, segregationist, unilateral approach that is not working for Jenny? How much will Jenny's family have to pay their high-priced lawyer to obtain a free (?) and appropriate public education for Jenny? What would Jenny's educational picture look like today if she had been in a general education classroom, supported by special education and literacy resources, from the very beginning? What did she do that prevented her being in such a classroom?

Where Jenny will receive her free, appropriate public education and what those services will be will now likely be decided in court. This is the sad reality for many students, their families, and their school districts today. In the meantime Jenny's educational clock is ticking and time is wasting.

Katie: Keeping the Faith

The concept of students not having to earn their way into learning situations but possibly doing something to earn their way out has important implications. If we are to follow the letter of the Americans with Disabilities Act, equal access needs to be provided to everyone in any community. People with disabilities should not have to earn their way into any public setting. A story about my niece Katie illustrates the point.

For years, both my nieces have been part of a local dance school troupe close to their home. Every year, the school presents a recital of over thirty dance numbers, featuring all ages of girls and women from the local and neighboring communities. My nieces perform in several numbers every year, meaning Uncle Pat has to be there from beginning to end, which I do gladly, because it means so much to them. I also present them with flowers after the recital and praise them for their artistic efforts.

In addition to performing her own dance numbers at the recitals, my older niece, Katie, has been an assistant teacher for the studio since she was eleven. She works with younger students to make sure they understand the steps, movements, and rhythms. And while they are on stage performing, Katie is in the wings, modeling the movements for them should they get nervous and forget where they are in the number.

During one dance recital, I noticed a young girl about four years old with cerebral palsy and leg braces successfully dancing along with everyone else in a big group number. I was mesmerized. I felt the effort of every step along with her. Her accomplishment was extraordinary. When the number was over, the audience applauded heartily, perhaps more warmly than for any number up to that point. My sister Vicky, Katie's mother, whispered that Katie had tutored the little girl with cerebral palsy, whose name was Grace. I was very proud that she had promoted the same type of inclusion in her own community that I strive for in mine, and that she did so naturally and without fanfare.

I asked Katie what she had done to teach and support Grace so successfully. She said she had spent many additional hours going over the steps with Grace and that she sometimes held Grace's hand when Grace was tired or fatigued. She also told me that no one had ever protested that Grace shouldn't be in the number or had been jealous of the extra attention she received. This is a reminder that attitudes are the greatest disability. Dancing with cerebral palsy and braces can be done if you believe it can be done.

When Katie found out that I was going to tell this story in this book, she mentioned that she is tutoring a new dance student, a young girl named Hanna, who has Down syndrome and is also deaf. Katie learned and is using sign language to teach and communicate with Hanna. I know Katie and Hanna are making a huge difference in each other's lives.

I am reminded of some wonderful words written by Ralph Waldo Emerson (2003):

> To laugh often and much, to win the respect of intelligent people and the affection of children, to earn the appreciation of honest critics and endure the betrayal of false friends, to appreciate beauty, to find the best in others, to leave the world a bit better, whether by a child, a garden, or a redeemed social condition, to know even one life has breathed easier because you have lived. This is to have succeeded.

If only we all did what Emerson articulates! Thank you, Katie, for helping others to be invited and included, to belong and succeed. You are an important inspiration for this book and have given me faith in the future generations that will support me when I am a senior citizen.

Chapter **Five**

Inclusion May Not Be Easier, But It's Better

Mark: A Defining Moment for Inclusion

Up until this year, fifth-grader Mark, a strapping lad who towers above his classmates, attended a self-contained classroom for students with behavioral challenges. This year Mark is receiving special education support in a general education fifth-grade classroom in his neighborhood school. This is something new for both Mark and his general education peers.

At the beginning of the year, one of Mark's new teachers, Gillian, concerned about his well-being, wondered how he would deal with his new expectations, and how she would feel prepared and equipped to support his learning needs. Since Mark has literacy challenges in addition to interfering classroom actions, a clear support plan needed to be created if his education was to be successful. Fortunately, Gillian was able to team up with special educator Marissa.

When Gillian and Marissa met with Mark's parents, Gillian confessed that although inclusion was new to her and she had very little training in teaching children with special education needs, the school was asking her to take this new direction. Wondering whether it would work in her classroom, she said she was grateful for Marissa's assistance. Gillian's lack of ownership and responsibility raised some eyebrows, and after the meeting Marissa assured Mark's parents that she would introduce both Gillian and Mark to inclusive teaching.

Gillian and Mark's initial relationship was fascinating to watch. Many times Gillian left Mark's support needs to Marissa or to part-time paraeducator Rosa, seeming to wash her hands of teaching him. Mark looked completely exhausted by the new demands and expectations being placed on him. And Gillian was strict about curbing Mark's interruptive classroom actions; she runs a tight ship, no exceptions. Marissa always asked to see Gillian's lessons, materials, and activities a week in advance, and together they made educational decisions about all the students in the classroom, including Mark.

One day a couple of months into the year, Mark clearly and correctly read aloud a paragraph from a book he'd chosen for language arts. Since Mark had never before read even one sentence aloud smoothly, this was a major first. Very excited by this breakthrough, Gillian called Marissa over to listen to Mark read. Marissa wisely commented that Gillian's instruction and modeling had been instrumental in Mark's achievement. Gillian proudly called Mark's mom and had Mark read to her over the phone.

This was a defining moment for both Gillian and Mark. Inclusion had come to mean something significantly different for each of them from when they began the year and neither one would ever be the same. They each had changed for the better because of the other, and inclusive education had achieved another well-deserved victory.

Components of Inclusion

Today, you could go to ten different school districts in neighboring cities or towns and ask their administrators whether they provide an inclusive education. Everyone will answer yes. Observing these supposedly inclusive classrooms, however, one might discover that inclusion means something different in each district!

True inclusion is the attitude that all students belong everywhere, with everyone else, in the school community. The strategy behind inclusion is to design supports—

True inclusion is the attitude that all students belong everywhere, with everyone else, in the school community.

innovative approaches to learning, differentiated instruction, curricular adaptations—for every student in the classroom, to include the entire spectrum of learners.

What are the essential building blocks that make an inclusive approach and attitude come to life? As a consultant to many inclusive education teaching teams, I have identified some best-practice components that help learners with disabilities thrive in an inclusive environment (Schwarz & Bettenhausen 2001):

> **T**he strategy behind inclusion is to design supports—innovative approaches to learning, differentiated instruction, curricular adaptations—for every student in the classroom, to include the entire spectrum of learners.

- Let students with disabilities attend the neighborhood school they would attend if they did not have those disabilities.
- Make them part of a general education homeroom.
- Never segregate them. When not in their regular classroom, they should be part of other general school environments.
- Carefully plan the course and progress of their education. A planning meeting should take place at least every other week.
- Solve problems as they arise.
- Introduce innovative, diverse learning strategies: universal design, differentiated instruction, cooperative learning, curricular adaptations, literature circles, educational technologies, cross-age peer tutoring and peer mediation.
- Create an educational team in which all members are equals.
- Cut down on unnecessary supervision and assistance by family members, professionals, and paraeducators (no learned helplessness).
- See behavior as a form of communication.
- Use everything in education's bag of tricks.
- Make it possible for students to join after-school clubs and take part in extracurricular activities.
- Be committed to making it work.

Let's look at each of these practices individually.

Attending the Neighborhood School

Most students who live in a community over a period of years are educated with an ongoing group of their neighborhood peers. I attended the same school from first through eighth grade and for the most part had the same classmates during those eight years. Attending a neighborhood school offers many opportunities, supports, and benefits, including social relationships: students know and help one another and develop deep, lasting friendships.

Having a General Education Homeroom

A general education homeroom conveys that all students in the school community are equal members with the same opportunities. If students with diverse educational needs are not in the classroom with the general student body, we encourage a we-they mentality that negates the inclusive sense of "us" that we are trying to create.

Avoiding All Instances of Segregation

Many school districts that claim to offer an inclusive education nevertheless maintain segregated classrooms. Children with disabilities are grouped in a separate homeroom, joining the general education school population only in certain classes termed the "specials" (art, music, physical education) or for lunch and recess and then without any planning or provision for special education support. Occasionally students with IEPs attend general social studies or science classes; almost never are they part of general language arts or mathematics classes. This is a mainstreaming model instead of an inclusive education model. Many school districts refer to mainstreaming as inclusion, but mainstreaming and inclusion are emphatically not the same.

Real inclusive education does more than just place students with IEPs in general education classrooms. Planning and support are part of the model. An inclusive education model opens other general environments to students as well: the school library, the computer lab, the gymnasium, and the lunchroom. Individual instruction from a special educator does not need to take place in a segregated environment. The library, a general study hall, or a resource room for the whole school are reasonable places in which *all* students can study, learn, and grow.

Planning, Planning, Planning

I've already said how necessary joint cooperative planning by general and special educators is for inclusive education to be successful. The planning guidelines outlined below have been adapted from my wonderful former doctoral officemate and friend, Alice Udvari-Solner (1995).

- Identify universal and differentiated instruction opportunities for all students within the lesson.
- Decide which individual educational goals need to be emphasized.
- Articulate the expectations for each student's performance.
- Determine the content of the activity, theme, or unit of study.
- Determine what and how to teach as a team.
- Determine how students with special education needs can actively participate and achieve the same essential outcomes as their general education classmates.
- If any student cannot achieve the same outcomes, select or design appropriate adaptations:

    Rearrange the instruction.
    Reformat the lesson.
    Use student-specific teaching strategies.
    Emphasize specific curricular goals.
    Adjust the physical and/or social classroom environment.
    Design more accessible materials.
    Supervise the student's work more directly (but still naturally).

- If the above strategies are not effective, design an alternative activity, preferably with other students from the inclusive classroom in a heterogeneous manner.

Solving Problems

I tell students who take my collaboration course, "It's not being problem-free that makes us effective teachers, it's being able to solve problems." Any educational innovation is going to involve certain problems—all change does. The important thing is to solve these problems. I have seen a variety of problem-solving formats, some detailed, others basic. My favorite approach is captured in the acronym SODA:

S = Situation:	Identify the problem that needs to be addressed.
O = Options:	Brainstorm potential solutions for five or ten minutes. Include all ideas that come up; don't dismiss any.
D = Decision:	Pick what you think is the best solution and start there. (Hold the other solutions in reserve just in case.)
A = Assess:	Create a way of evaluating whether you have solved the problem successfully.

With a successful and streamlined problem-solving approach like this, educational teams can take on any problem or challenge efficiently and successfully. No problem is too big.

Using Innovative, Diverse Learning Strategies

All classrooms need to be exciting, inspiring, thought-provoking, enlightening environments for every student. Teachers who use universal design, differentiated instruction, cooperative learning, curricular adaptations, literature circles, educational technologies, cross-age peer tutoring, and peer mediation are preparing their information-age students for success in living, working, and playing in their community.

Making All Team Members Equal

The adversarial mindset of schools versus families needs to stop. We must all work together as a collaborative, cooperative, progressive team to educate each student effectively. Students must have a role in making decisions about their education if they are to become citizens who advocate for themselves and determine their own appropriate actions. Family members must be seen as the experts that they are: they are responsible for their child the other eighteen hours of the day. If we all embrace what we bring to the table in a spirit of interdependence, we can change the world for our students.

Doing Away With Unnecessary Supervision, Assistance, and Learned Helplessness

Since the worst disability of all is learned helplessness, the best gift that can be given to a student with a "possibility" is independence! This means not doing anything for the student that he or she can do himself or herself. As the student gains more skill and moves toward greater independence, team members reduce their supervision and assistance.

Seeing Behavior as a Form of Communication

Team members who are most effective in dealing with students who exhibit interfering classroom actions see behavior as a form of communication. They make great efforts to understand and unravel what the student is trying to convey through his or her behavior. This is essential in situations where a student can earn his or her way out of an inclusive environment or situation with interfering actions to the classroom. This kind of understanding honors the student's perspective and prompts us to think about solutions rather than punishments.

Using the Whole Educational Bag of Tricks

The most effective teachers have a variety of tools, strategies, and techniques they can draw upon depending on what the student brings to the table that day. There is an old saying that "Imagination is more important than knowledge"; the educational bag of tricks is limited only by the creativity and ingenuity of the team members.

Providing Access to After-School Clubs and Extracurricular Activities

Students not only learn important skills and information from their academic classes, they also learn important life lessons from their peers within the social arena. Therefore, belonging to after-school clubs and taking part in extracurricular activities is an essential part of holistic learning. If a student isn't interested in any of the existing clubs, create a new one. For example, a former middle school student of mine, Caleb, didn't give a hoot for the clubs listed in the school handbook, but he was passionate about computer games. We started a computer games club with Caleb as the student sponsor, and it became a hit, thus greatly expanding Caleb's social relationships.

Being Committed to Making It Work

Both the professional and nonprofessional members of an inclusive education team have to believe in the model and in what they are doing for the student. Any team member who does not so believe is a weak link and may actively or passively sabotage the team's efforts. When the entire team is committed to making the model successful, they will win.

When judged by these essential components of inclusion, 95 percent of the schools who claim to follow an inclusive education model simply do not. Inclusion doesn't have to be all or nothing, however, on the road to change. Supportive leaders using these parameters as thoughtful and systematic guidelines can do wonders in improving the educational landscape for all.

Jack: Inclusion Is Better for Everyone

Let's look at a specific instance of one student with and another student without disabilities, each benefiting from an inclusive education.

Jack is an extremely intelligent fifth grader who has cerebral palsy. He uses a wheelchair equipped with a special laptop computer that "speaks" what he types in. This computer is an augmentative communication tool called a DynaVox. Jack has the intelligence of a typical fifth grader or above, but needs the support of his electronic system of communication, which takes added time to use (typing and programming, for example).

Jack is a fierce advocate for himself. When the state board of education ruled that students with IEPs did not have to take state-required tests, Jack insisted that he be allowed to take the tests along with everyone else. He wrote a letter to the board stating that although he was a student with an IEP, it was his right to take the required grade-level standardized test. He also requested that the test be programmed into his computer and that he be given the additional time he would need to take it in this format. The board agreed. As Margaret Mead so wisely said, it only takes one person to change the world. Fifth-grader Jack was able to change the state board of education! I am excited with the prospect of what he will do next.

Jack also decided that he wanted to run for secretary of the student council. With the help of his family and friends, he created campaign posters and hung them around the school. During the school rally where the candidates made their campaign speeches, Jack was on the stage with the other candidates, his campaign speech programmed into his DynaVox electronic communication system. As the school principal held the microphone up to the computer speaker, Jack said, "Hi, my name is Jack, and I want to be your student council secretary." Pandemonium erupted in the audience: "Cool, that computer with the voice is so cool—I'm voting for him!" When Jack won with more votes than all the other candidates combined, he was beyond happy. Another victory for inclusion, and everyone learned important lessons about belief, ability, assistive technology, and diversity.

Jack has many friends. His particularly good friend Chris, who is in Jack's general education homeroom, noticed that Jack needed help getting his coat put on: his arms were stiff and the coat wasn't flexible enough. Chris designed a coat for Jack that had zippers all the way down the sleeves, so Jack's arms didn't need to be bent to get his coat on. This was an incredibly thoughtful gesture. Jack was appreciative, his teachers were appreciative, and his parents were appreciative. One teacher recommended that Chris enter the coat into the State Young Inventors Contest. Chris did, and won a first place gold medal and a savings bond.

The lessons inclusion teaches go beyond the classroom into life.

The story of Chris and Jack is more proof that a well-planned and well-executed inclusive education is better for *everyone*. The lessons inclusion teaches go beyond the classroom into life. As pretty good kids like Chris and Jack become the pretty good adults of the next generation, we can all breathe a little easier about the world and our future.

Chapter **Six**

The Dignity of Risk Applies to All People

Ben: Portraying the Dignity of Risk

High school student Ben enjoys music, sports, and social events. He prides himself on being a self-starter and a young man about town. Ben also has Down syndrome. As part of his high school education, Ben participated in a work-study program and one semester was working at a local credit union. He received training and supervision from me as his special educator and also from a paraeducator.

Ben's educational team, which included Ben, his single mother (a great advocate), a speech-language specialist, the paraeducator, and me, decided that he should use public transportation to get to his job and back to school, since being able to use public transportation would let him make better use of the community after he graduates.

I began his training by riding the city bus with him from his home to his job each morning for a month. I showed him how to use a bus schedule and a transit system pass and when to ring the bell for his stop (when he saw the bright red sign atop a local theater). When we got off the bus, I taught him to cross the street with the walk lights, paying attention to his pace and the cars around him. It was most definitely teaching—teaching life!

When I was sure he was prepared and had data to demonstrate so, his mother agreed that Ben could try to make the trip by himself. For several mornings I got on the bus at the stop before his, hiding behind a newspaper so I could observe him unaware. He was fine. The next few mornings I followed the bus in my car. (Not a good idea. Never tail a bus that stops every two blocks!) Ben continued to do well: he was ready to make the trip without supervision. His mom was very pleased, and Ben was extremely proud of himself: he liked being independent. His mom started taking him places on the weekends, teaching him other bus routes.

About three months later, I got a phone call that Ben had been hit by a car while crossing the street on the way to work. I aged ten years on the spot. I went immediately to the nearby emergency room where he had been taken. Fortunately the car had only grazed him and he was not badly hurt: some bruises but no broken bones or internal bleeding. When the police investigated, we learned that Ben had correctly crossed the street on the walk signal. The car had made an illegal left turn into Ben's path.

After the accident, Ben sought recognition for what he had been through and said he wanted to be in a wheelchair. This made me feel even more guilty. Even though he had demonstrated that he could ride the bus and cross the street independently, accidents happen. What now? Should we no longer let Ben take the bus by himself? Did he need greater supervision? Ben's mother wisely decided that he should continue to ride the bus to work. The accident had been the fault of the driver of the car, not Ben's. He shouldn't have to give up his independence because of the driver's mistake.

The quality of his life is high, because a sensible parent and a caring educational team promoted his best interests in spite of adversity.

Today Ben is an employed, tax-paying adult who lives and plays in his community and uses public transportation to get around in it. He has countless choices and opportunities available to him every day. The quality of his life is high, because a sensible parent and a caring educational team promoted his best interests in spite of adversity.

The Dignity of Risk and Learned Helplessness

Ben's story is an excellent introduction to the concept of the dignity of risk. Anyone who crosses a public street is taking a risk. How does the dignity of risk apply to us? What does it really mean?

Remember when you were a little kid learning to ride a two-wheel bike and your parents took off the training wheels? Remember when they let go? Were you wearing a bicycle helmet? I wasn't. But even if you were, your parents took a risk by letting go, in order to let you experience the dignity of being able to ride a bicycle. In the name of special care, special safety, or special protection, we sometimes take the dignity of independence, choice, and freedom away from people with disabilities. We create a double standard, not letting them do things that nondisabled people take for granted, things that are often the rites of passage into maturity or adulthood.

> In the name of special care, special safety, or special protection, we sometimes take the dignity of independence, choice, and freedom away from people with disabilities. We create a double standard, not letting them do things that nondisabled people take for granted, things that are often the rites of passage into maturity or adulthood.

We do not want to promote unsafe situations, of course, but taking away a right from a person with a disability that everyone else shares would be terribly wrong. Educators and families need to teach safety and protective behavior to all children. Knowing how to be safe and how to protect themselves is the best insurance that persons with "possibilities" will be able to navigate the community and world wisely and well. Education and training open doors and permit opportunities rather than eliminate freedoms.

> Education and training open doors and permit opportunities rather than eliminate freedoms.

Lynda Atherton, a very wise parent and teacher I know, has two daughters, three years apart in age. Amy, the younger one, fun-loving and witty, has cerebral palsy and uses a power-operated wheelchair to get around her community. Lynda has told Amy's teachers throughout the years that 99 percent of the time what is good for her daughter without cerebral palsy is good for her daughter with cerebral palsy. She has learned from many experiences not to create double standards (see Chapter 3). This belief has provided a powerful impact! Amy now attends college, has a job, knows how to use a computer, spends time with a variety of friends, and has a boyfriend. Lynda has never accepted the status quo and has brought in a variety of consultants, experts, and visionaries who have helped Amy be able to live an effective life. Lynda's advocacy has revolutionized her local school system, which is now a welcoming place for students with identified disabilities. Lynda will never accept second best for either of her children. The possibilities for Amy continue to remain varied and open because Lynda believes in the dignity of risk.

Without the dignity of risk, the student experiences constant care and supervision, little opportunity to acquire important skills, and the promotion of learned helplessness. Learned helplessness is the worst disability of all.

Without the dignity of risk, the student experiences constant care and supervision, little opportunity to acquire important skills, and the promotion of learned helplessness. Learned helplessness is the worst disability of all. It is a more significant disability than anything involving learning intellectual, behavioral, cognitive, physical, sensory, or emotional challenges. It damages a person's confidence and independence and closes the door to many of the passages (Sheehy 1976) we typically go through in our lifetimes. These passages are important steps and experiences on the way to maturity. Passages are not easy for anyone, but they are critical to a functional, well-adjusted adulthood. Without the dignity of risk, we are robbed of the learning we need to grow. The myth that people with disabilities are perpetual children has been promoted by those who foster learned helplessness. In my quest of learning about disability and possibility, I have found it grossly wrong to treat anyone less than their chronological age.

What is learned helplessness exactly? Quite simply, it means that a person with a disability has learned to expect others to do things for himself or herself that he or she is capable of doing independently or perhaps in an adapted form with education and support. Typically, learned helplessness results from a belief, system-sponsored and reinforced during previous eras, that caring for people with disabilities in lieu of independence was the right way to proceed.

Parents who had a son or daughter with an identifiable disability were told by the medical profession that if they kept their baby, they would have to care for him or her for the rest of their lives. Many parents listened very closely to this advice and did their job too well, neither expecting nor encouraging their son or daughter to do anything on his or her own. Many educators also still promote learned helplessness with their students who have disabilities, which is a double whammy!

I am not blaming parents or educators, but rather stressing that important steps need to be taken to reduce and eliminate learned helplessness. The theme of the new era of dealing with disability is independence rather than care, a focus on possibilities rather than disabilities. Independence is not an all-or-nothing scenario; it is a journey that must be taken by any child on the way to adulthood. Let me show you three examples of the ramifications of learned helplessness and propose what should be done instead.

Julie: Protection Instead of Isolation

Julie, proud of her achievements in the classroom, is a second grader with mild cognitive challenges. She is a member of a general education classroom in her neighborhood school. She is quite allergic to bee stings, and spring has arrived in her community. Julie's father requests that since bees are likely to be buzzing about the playground, Julie be kept indoors at recess. Julie has had trouble developing the social relationships that most of her classmates are experiencing, and keeping Julie off the playground will greatly decrease her chance of playing with the other children and forming relationships.

What should be done instead? Julie and the playground supervisors should take protective action when Julie is on the playground: use insect sprays, avoid bee nests, and move away from areas in which bees are flying around. Julie does not have the option of living in a bee-free world, so teaching her to protect herself from them gives her a lifelong skill important for her own care and survival. Teaching her protective behavior is more powerful than denying her the important social experience of being on the playground.

Lindsay: Promoting Independence and Quality of Life

Lindsay, sweet and kind to all, is a high school student with learning disabilities, visual challenges, and asthma. Lindsay's mom doesn't want her to participate in any activity that involves physical endurance or stress. She also wants Lindsay to have a full-time paraeducator. The ramification of "too much care" has created a young woman who though innately very capable of initiating and performing a variety of skills is paralyzed from doing what she needs to do in order to function independently. Lindsay has a difficult time initiating anything. She fears repercussion if she tries anything on her own. Fear of failure is a disability in itself. She has learned to be helpless. This obviously will negatively affect her choices and opportunities as an adult.

What should be done instead? Lindsay should be taught what she can do to reduce her asthma symptoms and learn how to use her medication should she need it. She also needs more opportunities to try new things without the fear that she will be punished. And the support of her paraeducator should be gradually cut back while Lindsay is encouraged to initiate and participate independently in a variety of skills and routines. This will increase the number of decisions Lindsay makes about the quality of her own life. This greater independence will help her become a contributing member of her community, increase the quality of her life, and promote higher self-esteem.

Mick: We All Need Confidence and Competence

Mick is very social, is able to speak understandably, and is well liked by others. He also has good control of his physical movements. He also is a forty-year-old adult with cerebral palsy. Mick attends a "training program" at a "center" for adults with developmental disabilities, because he has been told over the years that he is quite disabled and should not be doing things that other people without cerebral palsy typically do. As a result, even though Mick would easily be able to live, work, and play in the community on his own, he:

- Continues to live with his family.
- Is unemployed.
- Goes only to the "activity center," staying at home the rest of the time.

Learned helplessness has taken away much of Mick's quality of life and will continue to deny him opportunities to grow and flourish.

What should be done instead? Mick needs more confidence and different kinds of experiences. He needs to learn to be on his own. He needs an opportunity to demonstrate his capabilities, to have a voice in the choices and decisions that affect his life. He needs to be empowered to exercise his rights and freedom. It is never too early or late for people to make changes and take steps toward improvement. He needs to be shown the activities in his neighborhood in which he can participate; he needs to be part of the life and pulse of the community.

Julie, Lindsay, and Mick are being or have been prevented from experiencing the rites of passage on their journey to adulthood. Our families and our society expect us to achieve these rites of passage. Yet all three of these people will not achieve the independence they so badly need if the dignity of risk continues to be denied them. They all have been taught some degree of learned helplessness, which is very difficult to unlearn. But if they don't unlearn it, they will not progress into full adulthood and become effective members of their communities.

The dignity of risk goes beyond individual people and applies to all the possibility studies depicted in this book. The dignity of risk is an attitude that must be championed by people with disabilities, their family members, their teachers, and other educational professionals. We must become "paradigm pioneers," agents of change promoting the dignity of all people in our currently ineffective educational and community systems. Many outdated attitudes, beliefs, and teaching practices regarding students with disabilities still prevail in school districts across America. Those who understand the dignity of risk can change the system and the world by thinking outside the "benevolence box" and persevering in a logical, step-by-step, yet progressive manner that invites everyone on the educational journey and helps everyone complete it successfully.

> Those who understand the dignity of risk can change the system and the world by thinking outside the "benevolence box" and persevering in a logical, step-by-step, yet progressive manner that invites everyone on the educational journey and helps everyone complete it successfully.

Schools that foster the belief that individuals with diverse "possibilities" are an attribute, are more similar to than different from the typical student, and are able to benefit from the same innovative and successful educational practices will successfully combat learned helplessness and promote the dignity of risk. Students with diverse "possibilities" offer opportunities for educational systems to be more divergent and creative in their thinking, planning, and delivery of practices and techniques. It is time for a new type of school system that promotes equity, dignity, and possibility, time to rise above mindsets that encourage mediocrity. Educators need to reimagine and re-create progressive school communities that serve all students. General and special education must both be reinvented, one diverse learner at a time. I hope this book will help you reinvent your educational system. Believe me, this can be achieved one learner at a time and the journey with all the hard accompanying work is well worth the effort!

It is time for a new type of school system that promotes equity, dignity, and possibility, time to rise above mindsets that encourage mediocrity.

Chapter **Seven**

Parents: The Gold Standard

Elizabeth and Trevor: Believe You Will Be Successful

Elizabeth is the mother of Trevor, a communicative and social five-year-old with cerebral palsy. Trevor is about to attend first grade at a school that is a model demonstration site for an inclusive education program. Trevor will be based in a general education first-grade classroom and benefit from the services of a general education teacher, a special education teacher, a speech/language specialist, a physical therapist, an occupational therapist, and a paraeducator. Trevor's preschool and kindergarten years were spent in a self-contained classroom for students with physical and cognitive challenges.

Elizabeth is unsure how she feels about Trevor's being in an inclusive classroom. The differences Trevor faces are these:

- He will be based in a general education homeroom rather than a self-contained classroom.
- He will receive most of his instruction in his homeroom.
- His special educator will lead the adaptive and differentiated instruction support process as they plan Trevor's activities each week. The general education teacher will submit lesson plans, activities, and materials one week in advance, and the whole team will decide whether and how the curriculum will be differentiated and adapted to support Trevor's needs.
- The speech/language, physical, and occupational therapists will work with Trevor in his general education classroom in

collaboration with his general and special education teachers. Jointly, they will apply their professional expertise to meet Trevor's needs in a general education classroom. This collaboration will also include Elizabeth, Trevor's mom.

- The team will write a joint individual education plan (IEP) for Trevor, not separate ones, so that everyone is on the same page.
- Trevor will be pulled from his general education classroom only when the specialized members of the teaching team are assessing Trevor individually. The information they gain from the assessment will be immediately applied to his general education classroom. Trevor's entire team will assess his first-grade goals and gains throughout the year.

Inclusive education is a new way of doing business for the entire team. Indeed, Trevor's new general education first-grade teacher, Ann, told Elizabeth that she didn't have any professional training for teaching students with disabilities. Elizabeth replied, brilliantly, "Ann, when I had Trevor, I can tell you for a fact that my husband and I had no training about having a son with cerebral palsy. We are getting by each day as it comes and what has worked most effectively is believing that we will all be successful. All I ask is that you believe in him; this will take you far in educating him."

"All I ask is that you believe in him; this will take you far in educating him."

Nevertheless, Elizabeth has some significant concerns of her own about the inclusive way of doing business:

- How will Trevor's IEP needs be met within a general education curriculum?
- With the related specialized service professionals now working in the general education classroom, will he have less time for speech/language, physical, and occupational therapy?
- What is her role and place in this new collaborative consultation team?
- How often will Trevor's teachers and the other team members communicate with her? After all, she has more questions and concerns than ever.
- Is inclusive education really a better way of educating Trevor, especially since the teaching team hasn't had much background in or experience with it?

- Will Trevor receive the amount of individualized attention and support he needs in a classroom of over twenty-five students? His classroom last year had only twelve students.

Elizabeth's concerns overwhelm her to such a degree that she contacts team members every day. Since these daily phone calls are time-consuming, the team looks for a more efficient means of communication and decides to try using a notebook that is always kept in Trevor's backpack. However, Elizabeth finds that the notebook doesn't really answer her questions about Trevor's schedule and therapy sessions. She wants more detailed information.

The team decides to use something they call the "IEP at a glance." The form, which is sent home every week for Elizabeth to review, includes Trevor's class schedule, which IEP goals are being met when, and a summary of Trevor's performance. This meets Elizabeth's concerns more clearly and directly: "I like the IEP-at-a-glance tool much better, because I know the team is attending to the IEP goals that we worked so hard to write. I was worried that with inclusion his teachers would not work on IEP goals anymore. Now I know they are addressing them effectively."

The team also sends Elizabeth a formal planning summary each week, which encapsulates Ann's lessons and activities and what the team will be doing to support Trevor effectively within this curriculum. Elizabeth appreciates this tool as well and has an open invitation to attend the weekly curriculum planning meeting whenever she wishes.

Something that happens during the year makes Elizabeth believe even more in the inclusive education approach. Trevor is invited to his first birthday party, a new experience not only for him but also for Elizabeth. Since Trevor uses a wheelchair, she goes with him to the party, which is being held at a place called Leaps & Bounds that has gymnastics mats, a sandbox of plastic balls, ropes to climb, and a variety of other games.

When Elizabeth and Trevor arrive at Leaps & Bounds, two girls immediately run up and exclaim, "Oh, great, Trevor, you're here!" They immediately steer Trevor's wheelchair away from Elizabeth and bring him over to the ropes course. Trevor can't climb the ropes on his own, but they help him reach his arms up to one, and

Trevor pulls on the rope with all his might! (Children will dare new things when encouraged by other children that they won't try under the supervision of adults. This is not meant to "dis" adults, but adults should remember this important fact.) Trevor is smiling, laughing, and truly having a grand time!

Elizabeth doesn't know what to do. She is frozen in place, watching her son having a wonderful time without her help and support: she isn't needed. She goes into the women's restroom and has a good cry, happy-sad tears that undo years of fearful perceptions she's had about Trevor, children, and society. She has witnessed firsthand the power of inclusion.

Elizabeth has continued to reflect on this experience. Because of Trevor's inclusion in school, she is now feeling included herself in the neighborhood. Children are coming to their door and asking Trevor out to play, which never happened while he was in a self-contained classroom. Elizabeth has met the families of Trevor's playmates and now knows many more people. Previously, she dealt mostly with the parents of the other students in Trevor's self-contained classroom—a sort of special education ghetto. Now she has a far wider, more diverse social network in the neighborhood, still seeing the parents from Trevor's past classroom, but so many others as well. It's all good, in her opinion.

In many American school districts, the family members of students with disabilities are looked on as the enemy.

This story of effective team collaboration and successful problem solving, unfortunately, is the exception, not the rule. In many American school districts, the family members of students with disabilities are looked on as the enemy. It is felt that they call or stop by too often, ask for too much (that is, they rock the boat), or, conversely, distance themselves too much and don't get involved at all. This mindset is handed down from generation to generation of educators and school leaders—they, after all, are the experts! But this is simply a blatant form of prejudice and one of the worst dysfunctions in our schools today.

Elizabeth had no training for caring for a son with cerebral palsy, but had him under her full-time care for the first five years of his life, twenty-four hours every day, and now is responsible for him eighteen hours every day. Just who is the expert here? There's only one answer, folks. Families know the most about their child.

There's only one answer, folks. Families know the most about their child.

Education professionals who do not embrace the expertise families have with regard to their own children should seek another line of work: they are *uneducated* about collaborative effectiveness and family dynamics. Families are, *by law*, essential partners in the educational process. Professionals who do not treat them as such should find a job that pays more and is less important! Families hold vaults of information about what works and doesn't work with their child. They know what they've already tried: the wheel does not need to be reinvented. Listening to them carefully is essential.

It is part of any educator's job description to work very hard at understanding the family dynamics that surround each student he or she teaches. It is hard to teach empathy, but that is most definitely the attribute needed here. Clearly, not all families are the same. There are many different types, and no family is going to be exactly like the one

It is part of any educator's job description to work very hard at understanding the family dynamics that surround each student he or she teaches.

we grew up in. But here's the big must: *Teachers have to like families to be successful and effective educators.* The adversarial mindset about families that is promoted in many school districts is a fossil and must be abolished.

Parents are not the enemy. The real enemy is attitude. I have long had a sticker on my office door that states, "Attitudes are the worst disability." This statement is true in many areas and walks of life, but especially so in the field of special education.

When individuals whose profession is to serve students and their families do not take responsibility for liking these students and families and being positive, helpful service providers, the educational team becomes paralyzed and ineffective, and education is no longer centered. The center of the education profession is the student, and the

The center of the education profession is the student, and the center of the student's life is his or her family. Making it work for everyone is our job.

center of the student's life is his or her family. Making it work for everyone is our job.

Brenda and Brian: Never Give Up

Brian, a middle-school student who is gifted in the areas of visual-spatial and bodily-kinesthetic intelligence, needs artistic and physical opportunities to express himself and be successful in school. Brian also has sensory integration dysfunction, a term taken from the American Psychiatric Association *Diagnostic and Statistical Manual of Mental Disorders* (American Psychiatric Association 2000). (I am never happy with the word *dysfunction*—do any of us want to be labeled dysfunctional?) Many have just dismissed Brian as simply having ADHD.

Brian also has an endlessly fertile imagination. One day I asked him and his mother, Brenda, to come to my office in an effort to find out everything I could about Brian so that I would be able to help him advocate for himself at school. Brian sat on the floor, and during our conversation (which he followed and participated in every step of the way), he took a smiley face and a toy cello from my shelves (I always invite my young guests to play with whatever intrigues them), configuring them so that the smiley face was holding the toy bow and playing the cello. A traditionalist would say that Brian was exhibiting noncompliant behavior by playing with things on the shelves and being on the floor during the meeting. An atraditional outlook recognizes that being on the floor and playing with these objects helped Brian process his thoughts! He was not interfering with what was going on and instead helped us accomplish more!

If Brian had the level of choice in school that he had in my office, he would have true success, empowerment, and achievement. True, we can't always choose what we get to do in school, but never being able to make choices promotes passivity, traditionalism, and sometimes rebellion. It is a crime to stifle someone with Brian's incredible level of imagination and creativity. It is also blatantly unnecessary. Brian is not the one who needs reform here.

Brenda has passionately and tirelessly advocated for Brian throughout his school career. Many of the traditionalist professionals she's dealt with have dug in their heels, closing their ears, minds, and hearts to what she has to say. Undaunted, Brenda has secured the resources of lawyers, advocates, and professionals who understand and believe in Brian. What might not be achieved if the professionals who understood and believed in Brian were the ones at his very own school? It's all in the way Brian is viewed and supported.

In spite of how Brian is viewed by school professionals, Brenda never gives up. She lives life to the fullest. She sends me inspiring e-mails about the power of people, how it only takes one person to change a system. She lives everything she says and promotes. Brenda and Brian's story reminds me of this poem by Mayer Shevin (1987), which is one of my favorites of all time for illustrating the importance of how we view a person:

The Language of Us and Them

We like things
> *They fixate on objects*

We try to make friends
> *They display attention-seeking behaviors*

We take a break
> *They display off-task behavior*

We stand up for ourselves
> *They are non-compliant*

We have hobbies
> *They self-stim*

We choose our friends wisely
> *They display poor peer socialization*

We persevere
> *They perseverate*

We love people
> *They have dependencies on people*

We go for walks
> *They run away*

We insist
> *They tantrum*

We change our minds
> *They are disoriented and have short attention spans*

We are talented
> *They have splinter skills*

We are human
> *They are . . . ?*

Even though Brian and Brenda continue to face an uphill climb within this country's traditional school systems, I remain very excited about Brian's future. I most definitely want him to get through school successfully. I know someone out there is going to see Brian's brilliance, understand what he is all about, and value him. He will succeed, perhaps even make millions of dollars with a creative idea. He is on the fringes of the paradigm, very out-of-the-box in his thinking. Those of you who now work with Brian and don't believe in him or refuse to adapt things to make education work for him, be warned. You will be blinded by his dust later. You will say proudly that you knew Brian, but he will likely choose to forget about you. Fortunately, Brian has also had teachers that he will never forget. I am hoping many of the people who are reading this book are cut from this latter cloth. It is up to Brian's teachers to work successfully with Brian and Brenda and make their school world a better place.

Tonya and David: Families Are Our Most Valuable Resource

A final story about trusting and working with parents. David is an animated high school student with significant learning disabilities. His mother, Tonya, is a single parent who works a double shift in a pharmacy and lives with her family on Chicago's west side. The staff at David's high school assumed that because Tonya had never attended meetings about him, she did not want to participate. When I became a consultant to the team, I introduced the Mcgill Action Planning System (MAPS) (Forest and Lusthaus 1988) in an effort to see that David would have employment opportunities and the chance to participate fully in his community when he graduated. MAPS starts with six questions:

- Who is David?
- What are David's interests and strengths?
- What are David's greatest challenges?
- What is the dream, the desirable future for David?
- What is the nightmare, the future to be avoided for David?
- What are David's greatest needs?

An essential part of MAPS is the participation of family members, relatives, and friends. It was therefore critical for David's family to be part of the process. (Families who have been part of MAPS report that they have never felt so included and valued. The process is a great equalizer in the divide between professionals and family members.) When I reminded the professionals at David's school how important it was for his mother and other intimate people in his life to be involved in the planning process, they told me, "We've never been able to get his mother to come to a school meeting. Why don't *you* ask her?" I said I would. They said, "Good luck."

The first time I called David's home, his older sister answered the telephone. I told her who I was and that I was trying to schedule an important meeting about David's schooling. She said their mother was working at the pharmacy and gave me the phone number there. I called, and spoke to Tonya on the first try. She was warm and apologetic. She told me that as a single parent she worked double shifts and that, in the past, meetings had been scheduled at times when she couldn't attend without losing her job. I asked what time would work for her. She said either very late on a Friday afternoon or early any weekday morning. Then she immediately apologized, saying she knew these were not typical school hours. I said we were flexible and would make one of these times work. When I told her that our MAPS planning of David's educational program would be greatly enhanced if his relatives and friends were involved, Tonya said she would host the meeting in their home and invite other family members.

David's classroom teacher and I went to David's home on the west side of Chicago early on the appointed Friday evening. When we walked in, I was amazed by the sight of *twenty-five* relatives and friends. People were upbeat and eager to contribute to the plan for David's future. Afterward, there was a celebratory dinner to which everyone was invited. I most definitely stayed. It was the best MAPS I have ever facilitated, and I've done lots of them! The people who attended the meeting had ideas about apprenticeships, work study opportunities, and places David could work (several volunteered their own businesses).

The meeting opened many doors for David and accomplished what it set out to do—fulfill dreams and create a desirable future. Today, David is employed at the same Chicago hospital at which an uncle who took part in the MAPS meeting is employed. One of the other major accomplishments of the meeting was the lesson that it taught the school professionals: sometimes we make assumptions and misinterpret the lack of family involvement as a sign they do not care. We need to look for creative options when solving these kinds of problems. All it took was for David's mom to suggest a time that worked for her and the family and for us to honor her needs and preferences. Building a bridge to communicate, listen, understand, and meet the needs of the family achieved great outcomes for David. Isn't that the hope and dream of education?

The stories in this chapter clearly show that we need to promote collaboration and empathy with parents in teacher training and professional development programs. Families are our most valuable resource. When I was taking special education methods classes, one very significant assignment was to stay overnight with a family who had a son or daughter with a "possibility." The parents with whom I spent time worked extremely hard on behalf of their son with disabilities and their other children and were positive and upbeat about it. It was an eye-opening moment in my professional development, and a major driving force behind this chapter.

The adversarial mindset between educational professionals and families must go. This is not an avant-garde idea. It just means that we must promote collaboration among all members of the educational team and value parents and family members as critical members of it. It is much simpler than one might think. The hardest part is breaking down the traditional, outdated us-versus-them barriers between educators and families that so greatly damage students and hold everyone back. It starts with each and every one of us looking within and putting ourselves in the shoes of the families with whom we work, using the power of empathy to create effective relationships and provide quality professional service to all our students and their families. That is, after all, the purpose of our life's work.

Chapter **Eight**

Get Rid of Labels

In my undergraduate teacher training program, the great moment arrived when I had finished my course work and was ready to begin student teaching. I was very excited: this was the last hurdle to clear before being certified and facing my own classroom of students. All the hard work was about to pay off!

But I was horrified when I discovered that I would be student teaching in the very high school I had attended! I'd be sitting in the teachers lounge with people whose classes I'd attended only four years earlier. I'll never forget walking down the halls on my first day. A number of my former teachers asked, "What are you doing back here?" and the looks I received when I told them were priceless.

My first few days were taken up with introductions and by observing in resource, self-contained, and general education classrooms. Assigning my responsibilities, my cooperating teacher, Jeanne, decided I would learn a lot by spending second period every day working individually with a boy whom she termed the toughest student in the school. Welcome to student teaching!

Nick: Beating a Self-Fulfilling Prophecy

Nick, a creative thinker, had been tagged with almost every label in the book (LD, BD, and more). He was failing every class—except math, because he liked his math teacher. He went to class when he felt like it and was often out on the school grounds smoking pot with his friends.

The first day I met with Nick, he arrived ten minutes late, reeking with the smell of pot. I was only four years older than Nick, and he seemed to feel comfortable talking to me. He said that none of the teachers knew how to teach except Mr. C. (the math teacher). He told me his father was always on the road. He said his grandfather drank all the time and became mean when he did, so Nick didn't want to hang around at home much. Nick did not have any books with him. He did not care about homework or remember what had been assigned the previous day. (So much for homework review.) It was obvious Nick needed to get to know me and adjust to this new experience. We would find our way together.

My instincts paid off. I was surprised and pleased when Nick arrived on time the next day. He told me about a fight he was having with another student in his crowd. He talked more about school: Mr. C. was getting a little harder on him, but Nick would still do things in math. I suggested that if he had homework he needed to complete for Mr. C., we could work on it during the period. He said homework was not important, that it wouldn't make a difference in what he did after high school.

I jumped at the lead he'd given me: "Nick, what do you want to do after high school?" He answered, very matter-of-factly, "I'll be a truck driver like my dad." Excellent, we now had something to work for and move toward. I asked him whether he knew what it took to be a truck driver. He didn't have a clue about what it took to get a trucker's license. Since Jeanne had told me I could set some priorities for the period, I put myself on a limb and said we'd find out—a defining moment for both Nick and me.

Nick arrived on time again the third day—the first hurdle had been crossed, he was showing up! As I was planning the evening before, I thought we would start by creating Nick's resume, since it involved writing for a real purpose. At first Nick demurred, but I stressed that people who applied for a job needed to have a resume. It was a tool for him to get where he wanted to go. So during the next couple of weeks, we worked on the resume.

(I did ask Jeanne whether working on the resume was okay. She replied, "Anything that gets Nick in school and working appropriately is acceptable." I was wise to get her blessing, because another special education teacher, whose class Nick never attended, felt writing a resume was not part of the curriculum. Since Jeanne was Nick's case manager, however, her endorsement ruled.)

After finishing the resume, Nick and I planned our next steps. We decided to send away for information about the program and the admission requirements of a nearby truck-driving school. I also thought we should visit the school in person, but I needed to find out whether I could take Nick out of school to do so. Again, Jeanne supported our visiting the school (I'm grateful to this day), while the other special education teacher thought it was a horrible idea: "Think of the responsibility, think of the liability and other safety issues." But Jeanne said we could go as long as I filled out a field trip form. I got the form and filled it out that very day.

The following week Nick and I visited the trucking school, successfully navigating public transportation to get there. Once we arrived, he was like a kid in a candy store. I had never seen him so lit up and excited. He was mesmerized as we watched a student drive through an obstacle course. There was no doubt in my mind that he was passionate about achieving his chosen vocation. During our tour, he greeted everyone with "Hey, man," and a smile. He fit in because he wanted to be there.

After the tour we sat down with one of the administrators to discuss admission requirements. One of the first was that he needed his high school diploma. This was another defining moment: now he had a major reason to finish high school. I knew our second-period sessions would take on a new urgency.

Back at school, I excitedly told Jeanne what had happened. She was extremely pleased, repeating, "There you go!" I also suspected she was going to enjoy sharing this success story with the other special education teacher. There was definitely a little of the rebel in Jeanne, which is probably why we got along so well. Having a kindred spirit during a stressful time like student teaching is priceless.

My next step with Nick was to find out from each of his teachers what it would take to get a passing grade in the class. Nick had a lot of catching up to do! Second period was going to make the difference in achieving his purpose in life. (He was also going to need to spend one or two more semesters in high school finishing his requirements.) It was a delight to see him start bringing books to second period.

I am happy to be able to report that Nick did become a truck driver like his father, continuing the family tradition. All it took was giving Nick a reason to attend school. We made education real for Nick (something discussed in more detail in Chapter 9). We also declassified Nick in many ways. Note the labels he'd been given:

- A student with behavior challenges.
- A student with learning disabilities.
- The worst student in the school.
- A drug addict.
- A student unable to learn.

These labels served no meaningful purpose. It was time to view him as capable of learning and let him have a stake in the process. The results were splendid! Isn't the so-called worst student in the school supposed to become a dropout? Nick was not part of this self-fulfilling prophecy; he beat the odds. I needed to believe in Nick and teach him how to believe in himself.

Franklin: Self-Advocacy Stamps Out Labels

Franklin, a big sports buff who had been given the label *autistic*, communicated some interesting things when he moved from a self-contained classroom to an inclusive school, sometimes kicking people or pulling their hair. Just what he was communicating needed some investigation.

Observing Franklin, we came to realize that he engaged in these "interfering actions" in situations that were uncomfortable for him, that involved new people, places, or expectations. (Being reluctant to change has been identified as a characteristic of autism.) We taught Franklin that instead of kicking or pulling hair, saying "I need a break" was an acceptable (and adultlike) way for him to get relief from new, stressful situations. We unraveled the communicative intent behind his behavior and created a replacement behavior that was purposeful.

Franklin was also about to make the transition from elementary school to middle school. His current and future educational teams knew that a lot of change was about to enter his life and would likely make him feel uncomfortable. We needed a plan to help support him, to orient him to the middle school and all the changes that would be taking place.

The year before he was to start middle school, we took Franklin to his future school during nonschool hours, when there were few students and staff members there. Because he was a big sports fan, we started by letting him go to the gymnasium and shoot some baskets. Afterward, we went to the cafeteria, where Franklin used the vending machine to get a can of soda. This was an excellent first step from which we could build.

The next time we visited the middle school with Franklin, we came on a day when only teachers were present. He met a couple of them, and we repeated the basketball and soda routines. We also brought along a padlock so Franklin could practice locking and unlocking a metal locker, another new experience. This step-by-step approach proved to be successful once again.

We also created a film about the middle school for Franklin. The footage began with the principal greeting Franklin from his office: "Hi, I'm Mr. Anderson, the principal of Central Middle School." Next, each teacher he would have as a sixth grader greeted Franklin from his or her classroom. We filmed coaches and physical education teachers in the gymnasium and cooks and servers in the cafeteria. We also filmed someone locking and unlocking a padlock on a locker. Franklin, by choice, watched the film every day during the summer before he was to attend the school.

On the first day of school, Franklin displayed none of his former adventuresome behaviors. Nor did he hit or kick during the first week, the first month, the first semester. It was wonderful. The school visits and film were very successful tools in helping Franklin cope with change. In fact, the school district was so excited by the success of the film, they decided to create an orientation film for *all* upcoming sixth graders! Franklin paved the way for districtwide change.

After school had started, we continued our journey of finding the right supports and opportunities for Franklin, who had been labeled:

- A student with autism.
- A student with behavioral challenges.
- A student with cognitive challenges.
- A student with communication challenges.
- A student who was difficult to teach.

These labels were not helpful in any way in discovering the best manner and system of successfully supporting him. Instead, we used the MAPS planning process (defined in Chapter 7) to examine his greatest needs. His greatest need was for social relationships. It was the top priority of his mother. Several supports, related to his being a sports buff, were arranged to help Franklin develop social relationships:

1. During homeroom, Franklin and two general education students were responsible for keeping the school's sports bulletin board, next to the doors to the gymnasium, filled with current school, local, state, and national sports articles.

2. These students were also the equipment managers for the school's major sports teams and therefore considered members of the teams. They made sure all the necessary sports equipment got to the practices and games, gathered up the equipment when each practice or game was over, and inventoried everything to make sure all the equipment had been returned. (Besides being a social opportunity, this responsibility helped Franklin develop a vocational skill.)

3. Franklin got to attend Michael Jordan basketball camp in Chicago. There is worldwide prestige in attending this particular basketball program. Franklin taught Michael Jordan and the basketball camp personnel about autism, and they taught him how to perform basketball drills—a win-win situation for all.

Franklin is attending college these days, is working, and has a girlfriend! There are adventures, but he has learned to be a self-advocate through the wonderful education he has received from his mother and his teachers.

Would the Artist Formerly Known as Special Education Please Stand Up?

Special education is full of labels and classifications. (I'm grateful to Karen Kaminsky for coining the above heading.) When someone is referred for possible special education services, he or she is tested and assessed. If the student qualifies for services, he or she is classified and given a label. The label is required for the school district to receive funding for these services from the state.

Difficulty arises when these labels are widely and openly used throughout the school day. Doing so creates unnecessary (and detrimental) barriers, as Doug Biklen (1992) discovered in his research on schools without labels. Labels defeat the purpose of individual educational programs and are one of the primary reasons that students with special education needs continue to be segregated. Students with special education needs who deal only with other students like themselves will very likely never have the performance models they need in order to learn and grow.

The mentality of "Let's put the students with the same special education label all together" still runs rampant in today's schools. However, there are educational "delabeling" practices that advance equity in the classroom, practices that are eons ahead of labeling and segregation. Here are some of them:

- *Keep labels out of everyday school interactions*. Use them only to acquire needed funding reimbursements for special education services. This is part of the game and part of the system. (Reforming special education testing and funding deserves a book of its own!)

- *Provide diversity education for all students*. Everyone has a gift and everyone has a challenge. Teaching students about learning diversity in themselves and in others goes a long way toward fostering understanding. One way to do this is through Gardner's multiple intelligence model inventories, which allow every student to identify his or her particular strengths and challenges. Students can also discuss why having diverse talents is important in the world and how having to struggle in certain areas is a learning opportunity.

- *Everyone has the capability to be a peer tutor*. This is especially true for older students asked to guide slightly younger ones and for those with specialized skills and talents. For example, Sarah, a second grader who struggled with mathematics to the degree that it affected her self-esteem, was asked to be a mathematics tutor for kindergartners. Her brilliant teacher wanted to boost Sarah's confidence in math and thereby improve her self-esteem. It worked—Sarah strutted out of the classroom proudly proclaiming, "I'm a math teacher!" Or again, Ethan, a second-grade student with deafness and the support of his very wise teacher, became the sign-language tutor for his whole school. The students were mesmerized (and had a secret language by which to communicate with one another in the halls!). Ethan's own execution of sign language improved and he became a very popular student.

- *Well-structured cooperative learning breaks down barriers and combats segregation.* One component of cooperative learning is heterogeneous groupings. Diverse groups of students are able to fulfill a variety of specialized roles as part of cooperative teams. For example, Mark, a third grader with emerging communication, became the poster designer for his cooperative learning science group. He found pictures of electronics and appliances that used different currents, assembled them on a poster, and pointed to them when they were mentioned during the group's presentation. The poster was a hit and remained displayed in the classroom for quite some time. Everyone won!

- *It is essential for everyone to have equal access to after-school clubs and activities.* Earlier in this chapter I mentioned how Franklin performed successfully as an equipment manager for the sports teams at his middle school. It was a wonderful opportunity for him to be a meaningful part of after-school sports. In Chapter 5, I used the example of Caleb, a middle-school student with significant learning disabilities who sponsored a new (and very successful) after-school computer games club.

- *Resource rooms for all turn the segregation paradigm on its side.* Traditionally, resource rooms and resource teachers were only used by students with identified special education needs. But certain wise and innovative school districts now let all students use these services, to everyone's benefit. The room is no longer a segregated place for some, but now holds a service for all.

Labels and segregation—and the lack of opportunity they engender—hurt everyone. They dehumanize people with "possibilities" and perpetuate misunderstanding, poor attitudes, unemployment, and withdrawal from the community. We all lose out in the end when the talents, gifts, and skills of all community members are not used to the greatest extent possible. Schools that take progressive approaches like avoiding labels, providing diversity education for everyone, equitable peer tutoring, cooperative learning, equal access to after-school clubs and activities, and resource rooms for all break down traditional segregationist approaches and provide caring, creative, meaningful, and effective education for every student learner.

Schools that take progressive approaches like avoiding labels, providing diversity education for everyone, equitable peer tutoring, cooperative learning, equal access to after-school clubs and activities, and resource rooms for all break down traditional segregationist approaches and provide caring, creative, meaningful, and effective education for every student learner.

Chapter **Nine**

Make Education Real!

Jamie: Zero In on What a Student Does Best

Fourth-grader Jamie is a great fan of music and rhythm. He walks to a certain beat, constantly taps his foot and his pencil or pen, and settles into a cadence when pounding away at a computer keyboard. He is constantly in motion. Teachers have to remind him to curtail his pen and foot tapping when it becomes too loud. Jamie also has an iPOD, which he wears during his walk to school and immediately again at the end of the day as soon as he leaves the school grounds. (He would wear it in the school hallways if it weren't against the rules.) If you talk with Jamie about music, he tells you there's always a song playing in his head. According to Howard Gardner's (1983) multiple intelligence theory, Jamie is a true musical, rhythmic learner.

Jamie struggles greatly with spelling and knows it. He depends on and benefits from computer spell-check programs, but when he has to spell on his own during class, he is entirely unconfident, even fearful. This worries him, his teachers, and his family. Jamie and his educators need a technique, strategy, system, to make spelling work for him so that he can feel good about himself.

When Jamie enters fifth grade, he has a new general education teacher, Carter. Carter has learned about multiple intelligences in his teacher preparation program and wants to find a way to make his lessons, activities, and materials work for all his students. Carter tunes into Jamie's musical and rhythmic abilities immediately and gives him the opportunity to incorporate music and rhythm into his school responsibilities.

One day Carter has an idea that turns out to be a transforming moment for Jamie. Why not let Jamie apply a rap beat to the language arts/spelling words he's trying to learn? This will allow Jamie to apply his top strength to his most difficult challenge! Carter turns on the rap beat and gives Jamie the words to practice. Carter also lets Jamie take the test orally using the rap beat, so Jamie can spell each letter to the music. The results are remarkable. Not only does Jamie's ability to spell increase significantly, but his self-confidence and positive feelings about school greatly improve as well.

Later, whenever anyone asks Jamie which of his teachers made the greatest difference in his life, he always says Carter, because Carter brought music into the classroom and found a way to use music to make spelling easier and more fun.

Each of us wants to be the teacher who makes education real and workable, positively impacting students for the rest of their lives. That's why we go into education. Making education real and workable for all students is important, and there are as many ways of accomplishing that as there are students. Priorities need to be set for each and every student in order to create successful outcomes.

> **M**aking education real and workable for all students is important, and there are as many ways of accomplishing that as there are students.

Dylan: Don't Waste a Student's Time

Dylan, a lover of films and photos, was an Ohio sixth grader with autism for whom I conducted an independent educational evaluation. He was based in a self-contained classroom for learners with disabilities but attended general education classes in music and art and ate lunch with the general student body in the school cafeteria.

Since Dylan's school curriculum emphasized life skills, I decided to observe Dylan for an entire day, both in school and at home before and after school. His parents understood why I wanted to do this and welcomed me into their home at 6:45 A.M.! Dylan's morning responsibilities included helping prepare breakfast, setting the table, putting the dirty dishes into the dishwasher after the meal was finished, dressing himself, and taking care of his personal hygiene. After school and on weekends he was responsible for cleaning his room and vacuuming.

Pleased with the way Dylan participated in activities at home, I observed what his school day was like. The first period was held in the self-contained classroom. First, the students identified the month, day, and year and discussed the weather. Afterward, students reviewed their assignments. So far, fairly typical.

However, the next period, a class called domestic skills, was another story. All the students in the classroom, including Dylan, proceeded to prepare breakfast! I have a hard time hiding my emotions, so I know I had a surprised look on my face. Why was Dylan making another breakfast at school when he had helped make breakfast at home less than two hours ago? Considering the many educational priorities identified in Dylan's IEP and knowing that he learned less rapidly than other students, why was making another breakfast important? And what was Dylan really learning? That it was all right to make and eat two breakfasts every day? What a waste of time and common sense!

Obviously in this instance, school-home communication left much to be desired. If school personnel had taken an inventory of what Dylan did at home, they would have learned that he makes his breakfast there.

I tell Dylan's story to make an important point: the best time to teach life skills is when they naturally occur. Here are some examples of life skills and when they should be taught:

Life Skill: Food Preparation

When to Teach

In school, the only time students prepare food is during snack time (if applicable) or before lunch. But the truth is that most students in the general education classroom do not prepare food in school; they either make lunch at home or buy it in the cafeteria. Therefore, teaching children to make lunch, snacks, or other meals at home is the normal way to proceed. Teachers can suggest that families include their child in food-preparation activities at home and provide ideas about how to go about it. This is an example of collaboration, and wisely prioritizing what gets taught where.

Life Skill: Using Money and Purchasing Things

When to Teach

Money and purchasing skills should be taught when the student needs to use money to purchase something. There is no need for a special class in how to use money. The school's cafeteria, vending machines, and bookstore are all environments in which students can and will learn and practice money and purchasing skills. Once again, consulting the family is the best way to proceed.

Life Skill: Personal Hygiene and Restroom Skills

When to Teach

Ever gone into a middle-school bathroom between classes? They can be wild places! The boys' restroom is just as wild as the girls', and the same amount of primping takes place in both (don't ask me how I know). The best time to teach personal hygiene—washing your hands, checking your appearance, combing your hair, applying hair gel(!)—is when the student uses the restroom. If the public restroom is too busy a place in which to teach these skills, many schools have a single-occupancy bathroom near the school office. The goal is always for the student to successfully use any public restroom in the end.

Life Skill: Communication and Social Skills

When to Teach

Communication is an embedded life skill: we need to use it in all environments throughout the day. Therefore, speech should be taught when the student needs to communicate. There are many students with a variety of challenges whose educational goals include developing better communication skills. Many of them receive speech/language services as well. With the speech professional as consultant, speech skills can be dealt with throughout the day when the student needs to use them. (Of course, individual assessment is sometimes needed in order to know what to teach.)

Life Skill: Eating and Table Manners

When to Teach

Where do students eat in school? Usually in the school cafeteria. (Perhaps they also sometimes eat a snack in the classroom.) Considering some of the behavior that goes on in school cafeterias, it may seem humorous to advocate teaching eating and table manners there. But a session in a classroom on eating and table manners is essentially a waste of time. Students should learn and practice these skills in the school cafeteria, where they are used.

Life Skill: Time-Telling Skills

When to Teach

Telling time is another embedded skill. It is used at many junctures and in many places throughout the day. It's best to teach students how to tell time when time is important: when a class begins, how much time they have for lunch, or when an after-school club convenes. Practice throughout the day is essential.

Life Skill: Recreational Skills

When to Teach

Recreation is defined as activities you *enjoy*. What is recreational to me might not be recreational to you and vice versa. Wouldn't life be boring and not worth living if we did not engage in recreational activities? Schools have natural times for recreation: whole programs do not need to be built around it. A great way for students to experience recreation in school is by joining after-school clubs and participating in extracurricular activities. If no existing organizations or programs interest a student, one can be created around his or her interests. For example, I know of a school that created a book-and-film club around the interests of individual students. Everyone was invited to be a member. Websites such as www. sparknotes.com have typical books that are adapted for different understanding and challenge levels, so everyone could learn and participate in a book club or the classroom.

Some school classes and environments may be recreational for particular students, depending on the activity and the degree of choice they have over what they do. Physical education is one example. Another is home economics, for students who enjoy cooking and sewing. The school library, with its opportunities to read books, listen to music, and perhaps socialize quietly with classmates, is yet another. The lunchroom and playground are also potential recreational environments. There are many possible recreational opportunities within a general education context.

Life Skill: Vocational Skills

When to Teach
Vocational skills can be promoted in general education starting at an early age and continued throughout the school years. I love general elementary classrooms that have job boards assigning students responsibilities such as cleaning the tables, feeding the classroom pet, shutting down computers, bringing classroom attendance forms to the office, delivering milk, and passing out lunch tickets. Responsibilities like these promote elements of a work ethic, to include:

- Initiating a task on one's own.
- Increasing the amount of time spent on a task.
- Performing a task to quality standards.
- Increasing the speed with which one does a task.
- Taking pride in the work one does.

As students with cognitive challenges or autism get older, they tend more to be diverted into a life-skills-only curriculum. Life-skills-only programs are not necessary nor educationally relevant for anyone. Students who receive these programs are being highly shortchanged. If I were the parent of a son or daughter with autism or a cognitive challenge, I would want academics to be taught within inclusive classroom settings and life skills to be promoted during the natural times they occur. In other words, I would want it all!

The debate between whether to include a student with autism or cognitive challenges in general education environments or provide them a life-skills-only curriculum in self-contained and community environments could be simply resolved if we teach life skills only when they naturally occur and promote educational/curricular goals as well. Life skills need not interfere with inclusion; both can work hand in hand. If experiential skills are taught when the student needs to use them, they are naturally embedded throughout the day and do not interfere with general classes or curriculum.

Older students (including those with IEPs) may have certain in-school jobs when they are not in class and may also have after-school or work-study jobs. The student's and his or her family members' priorities and choices must be considered in order to determine a meaningful high school curriculum. For example, is the student going to college? (Students who have significant challenges can still attend college.)

Dylan's story is a tough one. His parents wanted him to have the opportunity for a general education; the school was adamant that he participate in a life-skills-only program. With a commitment to teaching Dylan life skills in the contexts for which they are needed, the district could also have promoted inclusive education. Dylan would have been getting a bigger bang for his educational buck, and his educators would have been making better use of his educational time.

Of course, this takes belief, skills, imagination, techniques, strategies, and a commitment to making it all work. It also means more teaching and promotion of skills throughout the day. Unfortunately, Dylan's team was not committed to making inclusion and life skills work hand in hand, the approach I recommended in my evaluation (I also included suggestions about how to bring this about). Instead, Dylan's school-based team sought out every excuse they could to not do so. Tragically Dylan's family ended up having to move to another school district to get these services; but happily, Dylan did end up getting them. The cost was great to Dylan and his family, as it always is when educators lose the spirit of putting the student first and making education work.

When considering the importance of life skills as students with challenges move up the educational ladder from elementary school through high school, we need to acknowledge that 50 percent of all students in general education do not go on to higher education. We want these students, too, to be employed, successful, and happy. Did their school system prepare them to be? Rather than touting test scores, grades, and academic statistics, why shouldn't school systems be made accountable for each student becoming a productive member of the community? This is a provocative question, but not so farfetched when you consider that for 50 percent of our students, high school is their last chance.

Educators hold a precious responsibility. Too many students have every right to say, "School failed me; I'm unemployed." Are we wasting our students' time by not making education a real enough preparation for life? The first line of the song "Kodachrome," by Paul Simon (1973), comes to mind: "When I think back on all the crap I learned in high school, it's a wonder I can think at all." Employers look for a number of essential skills in their employees: the ability to collaborate, solve problems, access information, apply technology, and use their imagination. Teaching students these skills in a diverse classroom through cooperative learning, peer tutoring (as long as everyone has the opportunity to be a tutor), peer advocacy, and student-directed projects is essential. There is also an increased need for experiential instruction within the community: opportunities such as work-study programs and business apprenticeships are very meaningful. High school work-study training is also a component of many special education programs.

Let's look at two learners who did not go on to higher education after high school but who benefited from a real education provided in an innovative, provocative way.

Justin: An Educational Wake-Up Call

Justin, a proud and manly high school student with Down syndrome and an IEP, had a work-study job at a local gourmet restaurant. Justin set the restaurant's tables for lunch and stocked the salad bar. He also helped prepare food in the kitchen when his other jobs were finished. He was reliable and dependable, had a positive and polite work attitude, and was well-liked by the owner and staff of the restaurant.

One day Justin's mother called me and told me she'd found his backpack full of straws from the restaurant. I said I would speak to Justin's employer. The next day, Justin's employer warned Justin about stealing from his place of employment. He told Justin that people lose their jobs for stealing. Justin nodded and said he would not steal again.

Unfortunately Justin did steal again. The employer really liked Justin and didn't want him to lose the job, so he decided to give

Justin a second warning. He also realized that the stealing couldn't go on. Together the employer, Justin's family, and I worked out a plan with the community police department: Justin would be put in jail if he stole a third time, not for a real criminal offense that would give him a police record but rather as a strong message that we hoped would finally hit home.

Justin did steal a third time and was taken for a ceremonial but sobering visit to the local police station. I feel odd about it to this day; however, let's characterize it as tough love. The outcome was successful. Justin has never stolen in the workplace again, and remains employed today. Putting Justin in jail was an out-of-the-box solution, but it taught him a very real and important lesson that I don't think he would have learned any other way. Stealing was compulsive for him, and he needed a wake-up call.

Ella: Sometimes We Need Tough Love

Ella was also in a high school work-study program. She did clerical work at a local insurance company, getting there by public transportation. Like most postpubescent young women, she was interested in men. At a bus stop one day, she said to a strange man, "I like your belt buckle."

Red flags were immediately raised by Ella's family and her teachers. They were worried that someone might take advantage of her. My belief in the dignity of risk was firmly planted by then, and I did not want her to stop getting to work independently. I said, "Why don't we teach Ella protective behavior?" Everyone agreed this was a wise idea.

However, teaching Ella protective behavior in school didn't seem to be making a difference in her life: she continued to make flirty comments to strange men. Ella's family members told the educational team that they'd witnessed several instances of inappropriate behavior when they'd gone places with Ella in the community. Obviously we needed a new plan for Ella to be more street smart, savvy, and wise.

We (the educational team and Ella's family) decided to stage an encounter that would dramatically demonstrate to Ella the need for protective behavior. We thought up a situation in which Ella's safety and protection would be compromised, wrote a script, and brought in an ersatz actor to help us. A teacher Ella did not know (he taught in another high school) would approach her in his car and offer her a ride and some candy. I would take it from there.

When Ella was approached by the teacher, she said, "All right!" to his offer of a ride and some candy and went happily toward his car. I stepped from behind some bushes where I'd been observing the scene: "Ella, don't do that, the man has a gun." There was a real-looking plastic gun on the front seat of the car, and it definitely shook Ella up. The other teacher and I got into a pulling match, Ella in the middle. Finally, I freed her arm from the other teacher's grasp and told her to run away. She ran so hard it was clear she felt she'd come within an inch of losing her life!

The great news is that Ella completely stopped her flirtatious comments to strange men in the community. In this second example of tough love, the scripted scenario brought home the point that she needed to be careful around strangers and protect herself from possible harm. Ella remains employed today, and her quality of life is excellent.

These two examples of tough love illustrate that we sometimes need to put longitudinal real-life priorities such as being employed and safe ahead of being nice. To this day, having Justin ceremonially locked in jail and providing the scare-tactics role-play scenario for Ella shocks me about myself. At the time, I had to put my own personality and style aside and do the right thing for these two students. Looking back now, I believe putting tough love to work was the right thing.

There are many things teachers can do to prepare students for life after school. It is never too early to start. Assigning students classroom duties teaches them job skills and a work ethic. Classroom structures that transfer increasing responsibility to students for their work, like goal setting, record keeping, monitoring, and evaluation (Zemelman et al. 2005), are also important components of any job or career. It's also critical to capitalize on a student's strengths. Pairing spelling and rap as an educational technique for Jamie was not magic, it was using Jamie's strengths within educationally sound practices.

Education became very real for Jamie when music and rhythm were paired with spelling and for Justin and Ella when they learned

> Teaching techniques for dealing with real life to all students is mandatory if we are to create a caring and cooperative next generation.

about the potential consequences of their actions in work-study programs. Teaching techniques for dealing with real life to all students is mandatory if we are to create a caring and cooperative next generation. Turning out responsible citizens who will make our future world a better place is what education should be all about. Let's just do it!

Chapter **Ten**

Disability Is Normal

— *Disability is an opportunity to search other hidden talents you have.*
Sam Sullivan, Mayor of Vancouver, BC
and Commissioner of 2010 Winter Olympics

Several years ago, I received a phone call from my friend Paul. He told me there was something he wanted me to see and asked whether I could meet him at an address a few blocks from my home that Wednesday at 11:00 A.M. A bit mystified, I said, "Sure."

I met Paul on Wednesday as agreed. He asked me to look around the building and give my opinion of what was taking place. I began walking through the building and saw people in some rear rooms using wheelchairs to get around. I also noticed a never-ending line of people in wheelchairs at the back of the building; they were waiting to use the bathroom. I walked through some more rooms in the building and discovered a computer and some books in one of them, but no one was using either the computer or the books.

I returned to the front of the building and joined Paul outside. He asked me what I'd noticed. I said, "I don't know if I came at the right time, but if you're in a wheelchair and in the neighborhood and want to wait in line to use the bathroom, it's the place to be!" Paul then told me that the people in this rehabilitation "center" were learning how to apply and interview for jobs. Thinking about the high unemployment rate for people with possibilities, I told Paul that made sense. I also asked him how many people had gotten jobs as a result of this training. He told me none ever had. (These people were between the ages of twenty-three and sixty-seven; some of them had been going to the "center" for twenty years.) I told Paul that didn't make any sense at all, and he shot back, "You want to do something about it?"

I bit and was given an office in the front of the building. Suddenly the line shifted from the restrooms at the back of the building to the door of my office. People were probably wondering, "Who is this person from another planet?" I listened to their life stories, many of them heartbreaking, painful, and depressing. I went home after my first day in that office and cried.

One day, a gentleman appeared at my office door. In a hoarse voice, he said, "I'm about the last person you would ever want to do anything with; my name is Bob, I'm sixty-seven, the oldest person here, and I want to tell you my story. When I was a little boy, both of my parents died in a car accident. Because I have cerebral palsy, and no one from my family could take me in, I went into a children's home. I now live in the adult version of that—a nursing home. But I have always known in my heart and my soul that I could go out there and work! Would you help me get a job?"

Fighting back my emotion, I told him, "Bob, let me take in that story for a minute. It's heart-wrenching. I will tell you what, however. I'm here to try to create new outcomes for people, and you have identified a very important one you would like to achieve. I'll put you at the very top of the list if you work just as hard as I do." Bob immediately replied, "I can do it, I can do it, I can do it!" I heard his voice echoing those words whenever I passed him or thought about him.

Whenever I try to help someone achieve an outcome such as employment, my first rule of thumb is to get to know the person, finding out what "wows" him or her in life. We should all have a job that we love to perform—think of all the time we spend at the workplace these days! Therefore, I had lunch with Bob. (I can find out much more about a person over lunch than by administering a huge stack of formal assessments.) Bob was full of stories, and one stood out. He told me he used to have his own front booth in the restaurant across the street from the nursing home, and everyone who came in knew him: "Bob, how's it going?" The restaurant was like home to Bob, where he felt a sense of family. But it had closed down. Then Bob said, "I want to work in a restaurant." I said, "Great, Bob, I wouldn't even eat these days if it weren't for restaurants!"

I told Bob I would like to schedule a person-centered planning meeting of people he wanted to invite who could help us plan ways he could find a restaurant job and perhaps suggest possible places or connections. I was alarmed to discover that Bob and the other regulars at the "center" had very few outside connections and relationships. I am not fond of the word *"center"* because what happens when people are put in these segregated places is that environment becomes the *center of their lives,* in lieu of being people out in the general world community. The center of a person's life should be his or her neighborhood and where she or he accesses family and friends. This was frustrating to say the least, a wake-up call for me in my attempt to be the innovator, and very humbling.

I told him, "Bob, let's take all of the things you have learned all these years in this place, walk out the door, and apply them to the real world!" Then I grabbed a *Chicago Tribune* and dramatically turned to the restaurant-employment section of the want ads.

In our quest to get job interviews for Bob, we soon encountered a Chicago legend—the Home Run Inn, a place where many baseball teams go for pizza after their games. It's popular and a fun place to eat. Bob got an interview with the manager, Jerry, who said, "Bob, four thousand carry-out and delivery pizzas leave this restaurant each week, and our kitchen personnel cannot keep up with the boxes that need to be folded and the napkin sets that need to be packaged. Is that something that you could do for us?"

Bob said, "I can do it, I can do it, I can do it."

Jerry told Bob, "I like that attitude," and got some boxes out for Bob to fold. I suspect that it took Bob at least three times as long to fold a box as a typical person in that kitchen, but it didn't seem to matter to Jerry. He said, "Bob, we're going to start you on the Tuesday and Thursday lunch shift; be here at 11:00."

At sixty-seven, Bob had his first job—as an assembler of pizza boxes! By sixty-seven most of us have retired, but Bob was not the "retiring" sort. He was jubilant, beside himself with happiness. He had achieved his goal!

Arriving at the Home Run Inn for Bob's first day of work, we went to the employee entrance at the back of the restaurant. Bob uses a wheelchair to get around, and we were happy to find that the back entrance was accessible: it had to accommodate the produce carts that came in and out of the kitchen. The ramp from the parking lot was steep, however, and Bob had to use every bit of strength he had in his arms to get up it.

When Bob entered the kitchen, every employee was looking at him. A man approached him and said quite loudly, "It's so sad, it's so sad." I immediately thought of Norman Kunc's Website. (Norman is a wonderful self-advocate for people with disabilities; if you ever have a chance to hear him deliver a keynote speech, don't miss it.) At one time on Norman's home page (Kunc 2006) there was a photo of himself carrying a sign that said, "Piss on pity!" That in a nutshell is the feeling people with "possibilities" have when someone extends sympathy about their disability. They want their disability to be viewed as just one more aspect of the many things that make up their life.

Fortunately the comment rolled off Bob's back. He went right to the work area Jerry had set up for him, saying "Hi" to people along the way. I was happy to see that the work area was right in the middle of the kitchen; Bob was a very social person, and I knew the location would serve him well. Bob immediately started to fold boxes, as everyone continued to stare.

Finally, Bob ran out of unfolded boxes. Instead of jumping in to help him get more, I suddenly became very interested in a form on my clipboard. My support would only help him for this one moment; how he and his coworkers dealt with this situation (something we call *soliciting natural supports*) was the important thing. Fortunately, almost immediately, a woman in the kitchen brought more boxes to Bob, introducing herself as she did so: "Hello, my name is Maria." I said to myself, *We're on a roll!* Bob thanked Maria graciously and continued to work very intently.

It was so heartening how Bob took to his job. He had to be told when to take a break; he would have been very willing to work straight through, no breaks, no lunch. I was impressed by and thankful for this amazing work ethic.

As Bob's shift came to an end, the "it's-so-sad" man approached him again. This time he made a very offensive, sexist comment, which I share only reluctantly: He said, "Bob, I'll get you a good woman after work." Was he thinking this would "cure" Bob or something? We had some work to do here surrounding belief and attitude!

Bob continued to go to his Home Run Inn job two days a week. One day I received a phone call from the nursing home's physical therapist, Regina. She said, "Pat, could you tell me what Bob does at his job, because he is doing things he has never been able to do before.

He is getting out of his chair and reaching for things." How should I handle this? I finally said, "Would you like to come and observe Bob at the job and offer your recommendations?" Regina said she would.

The following week, Regina stopped by Home Run Inn, where Bob continued his exceptional commitment to his job. Afterward she told me: "This job is helping him physically. I am very pleased with everything. I am going back to tell everyone at the home." We had the nursing home's Good Housekeeping seal of approval!

One day Bob asked me if I would take photos of him at work. I told him, "Sure," and brought my camera in the following week. Bob posed with some fifty people and wanted photos with me as well. Several weeks later, when I stopped by while Bob was working, he started waving something in his hand when he saw me. It was the nursing home newsletter. On the front cover was a photo of Bob and me. I told Bob, "It is wonderful that you are on the cover, but don't you think I'm a little young to be in a nursing home? What were you thinking?" Bob roared with laughter and showed the newsletter to everyone nearby.

When Jerry, the kind manager, hired Bob, he also inherited me. Every time that Bob would work, I would either stop by in person or phone Jerry to find out how things were going. "Is Bob going fast enough?" "Is Bob getting along with his coworkers?" "Is Bob fulfilling all your expectations?" "Is there anything we can do to make things better?"

After a few weeks of this, Jerry finally said, "Pat, shut up and get out of here! We have many people in our kitchen that come from tough walks in life. Bob has had a tougher walk than all of them, and Bob is the person who comes in every day, happy, smiling, thankful to have a job, and we even have to tell him when to take a break! Businesses pay big bucks to motivate their staff, and we have Bob! Plus he really likes our lunches here and he thinks the nursing home food sucks, so we want him here every day!" I said, "Jerry, I can't argue with that. But can I still stop by and have lunch with Bob once in a while?"

Why am I ending this book with the story of a sixty-seven-year-old man who never had a job and when he finally got one, it was assembling pizza boxes? Because Bob teaches us all some very important lessons. As he once said, "I waited sixty-seven years to get a job. Don't make anyone else wait that long."

Quality inclusive education for students in schools leads to a greater chance of quality inclusive community participation for adults.

Inclusive education is important for everyone and is a womb-to-tomb issue. Quality inclusive education for students in schools leads to a greater chance of quality inclusive community participation for adults. Bob never had the opportunity to be included in a general education environment; he went to a segregated school. He achieved his dream of employment in the end, but this would have happened much more quickly and easily had Bob been included in a public school.

Quality inclusive education means that:

- Everyone learns to work with one another in school, with the hope that everyone is learning to live with one another in the community.
- Everyone becomes educated about the diversity in their community. Experiencing diversity in school prompts students to support diversity in the community when they become adults.
- We increase the chance that *people with possibilities* will take on active roles in their community. They become employees, employers, neighbors, and friends along with their nondisabled counterparts. Our community becomes stronger, and we decrease the unemployment rate for people with disabilities. We use an untapped population of people who have much to offer the world.

We will all have a disability someday if we are lucky enough: old age.

Disability is part of the normal human experience. As I said at the outset of this book, we will all have a disability someday if we are lucky enough: old age. We will not be physically able to perform all the things we take for granted now. Inclusion teaches our children how to support others, and it will benefit everyone who achieves senior citizenship.

Bob's story teaches another important lesson as well. When someone asks me what is the most important job in the world, I do not say doctor (even though I know doctors are very important). I do not say lawyer (even though we know they are also very important, if in a different way). Every time I am asked what is the most important job in the world, I always answer teacher! Teachers are the people who hand out *life chances for everyone*. Teachers educate everyone from all the professions. Teaching is the most noble of all vocations. Teaching is also an incredible responsibility. Our society needs to value the fact that quality teachers inform and shape quality students who in the future become quality community members. This is what education is all about.

We all lack some kind of ability, and most certainly we all hold the realms of possibility within us. Bob's story shows us, in the flesh and blood of a living, breathing, human being, that disabilities hold no boundaries and can be gifts rather than stumbling blocks, as long as we believe in possibility and help others do so too. Now is the time for us all to join forces to make that happen. I am on that journey and would be honored if you would join me.

Works Cited

American Institutes for Research. 2004. What are we spending on special education in the United States 2002–03? *Advance Report No. 2, Special Education Expenditure Project*. Washington: American Institutes on Research.

American Psychiatric Association. *Diagnostic and Statistical Manual of Mental Disorders*, 4th ed. 2000. Arlington, VA: American Psychiatric Publishing.

Biklen, D. 1992. *Schooling without labels*. Pennsylvania: Temple University Press.

Brown, L., P. Schwarz, A. Udvari-Solner, E. Frattura Kampschroer, F. Johnson, J. Jorgensen, and L. Gruenewald. 1991. How much time should students with severe intellectual disabilities spend in regular education classrooms and elsewhere? *Journal of the Association for Persons with Severe Handicaps* 16(1):39–47.

Daniels, H., and N. Steineke. 2004. *Mini-lessons for literature circles*. Portsmouth, NH: Heinemann.

Emerson, R.W. 2003. *The spiritual Emerson: Essential writings by Ralph Waldo Emerson*. Washington, DC: Library of America.

Forest M., and E. Lusthaus. 1988. *McGill Action Planning System for future planning*. Canada: McGill University.

Gardner, H. 1983. *Frames of mind: The theory of multiple intelligences*. New York: Basic Books.

Internal Revenue Service. 2005. http://www.IRS.gov (February, 2005).

Kluth, P. 2003. *You're Going to Love This Kid! Teaching Students With Autism in the Inclusive Classroom*. Baltimore, MD: Brookes.

Kunc, N. 2006. http://www.normemma.com

Lavoie, R. 1998. *How difficult can this be? The F.A.T. City Workshop*. Washington, DC: WETA.

Roessler, R. 2002. Improving job tenure outcomes for people with disabilities: The 3M model. *Rehabilitation Counseling Bulletin* 45(4). 207–212.

Schwarz, P., and D. Bettenhausen. 2001. You can teach an old dog new tricks. In *Restructuring for caring and effective education: Piecing the puzzle together*, 2nd ed., ed., R. Villa and J. Thousand. Baltimore: Brookes.

Sheehy, G. 1976. *Passages: Predictable crises of adult life*. New York: Bantam Doubleday.

Shevin, M. 1987. *The language of us and them*. http://www.shevin.org

Simon, Paul. "Kodachrome." *There Goes Rhymin' Simon. New York*: Columbia. ℗ 1973.

Udvari-Solner, A. 1995. A process for adapting curriculum in inclusive classrooms. In *Creating an inclusive school*, ed. R. Villa and J. Thousand. Baltimore: Brookes.

U.S Census Office. 2000. *Statistical Portrait of the Nation's Hispanic Population*, by B. Guzman. United States Department of Commerce News. Economics and Statistics Administration. Washington DC: Government Printing Office.

Villa, R., and J. Thousand. 2001. Setting the context: History of and rationales for inclusive schooling. In *Restructuring for caring and effective education: Piecing the puzzle together*, 2nd ed., ed. R. Villa and J. Thousand. Baltimore: Brookes.

Walker, R. 2004. *Unemployment rates tell half the story*. Virginia: Newsday.

Wikipedia Encyclopedia. 2006. Chicago, Illinois: http://en.wikipedia.org/wki/Chicago. March 14, 2006.

Zemelman, S., H. Daniels, and A. Hyde. 2005. *Best practice: New standards for teaching and learning in America's schools*, 3rd ed. Portsmouth, NH: Heinemann.